GOD Loves MOMS

By Christina Hergenrader

Twelve Lessons about God's Mercy

CONCORDIA PUBLISHING HOUSE · SAINT LOUIS

Copyright © 2011 Concordia Publishing House
3558 S. Jefferson Avenue, St. Louis, MO 63118-3968
1-800-325-3040 · www.cph.org

Manufactured in the United States of America

For Catie: I pray I'm your **INDEPENDENT** Mom.

For Sam: I pray I'm your *SiLLY* Mom.

For Ellie: I pray I'm your **Reliable** Mom.

For Nate: I pray I'm your *Energetic* Mom.

Table of Contents

Before You Begin This Bible Study

Hello, sister in Christ.

I'm so glad you're here.

We probably haven't met face-to-face, but here, in this study, we have the chance to become friends. Friends are those people we're vulnerable with. They are people who see us without our emotional mascara and wrinkle cream. It's always a risk to show our true self to someone else, isn't it? For me, going public with my insecurities and shortfalls is even scarier than facing the world sans mascara—that's really something, coming from a woman who needs the heavy-duty stuff to avoid looking twice her age.

Dear friend, through the pages of this book, you and I will look at twelve women of the Bible—twelve moms—and get to know them and their deep vulnerabilities. If we had lived with them thousands of years ago, if we had carried water and raised children elbow to elbow with them, we may not have been close friends. We might not have appreciated their vulnerabilities. But today, we have an advantage—we know the rest of their stories. In God's Word, we see that these mothers were common women with deep insecurities and fears. We'll meet women who felt painfully inadequate because they couldn't get pregnant, who plotted and cheated, who lost children, and who shared their husbands. And because each of them was a mother, each was especially vulnerable.

Isn't that what motherhood is? A risk, a lifetime exposure to insecurities, fears, failures, and love? Although we are daughters of our heavenly Father, there are times when we also feel vulnerable. So often, we try to hide our insecurities from Him, but He sees straight into our hearts. And despite knowing our sins, God loves us—each of us. He's given us His Son, the salve that heals our festering fears.

This Bible study is about more than twelve stories of moms in the Bible. *God Loves Moms* is about the work of Jesus in their lives and ours. When we see the vulnerability, pain, and sin of these mothers, we also see the story of salvation through our Savior.

What's your story? Will you make yourself vulnerable to learn from these moms? Will you use these stories to take a closer look at your own life? More important, will you draw something from these women's stories to help you embrace the life-giving security God offers you through His Son?

Come along, friend. Come along, sister. Let's see what we can learn about our Father and how much He loves each and every kind of mom.

Thanks for joining me,

Christina Hergenrader

Suggestions for Small-Group Participants

1. Begin small-group time with prayer.

2. Everyone should feel free to express her thoughts. Comments shared in the small group should remain confidential unless you have permission to share them outside your group.

3. If your meeting time does not allow you to discuss all questions for the week, the leader should choose the questions most meaningful to the group.

4. Close by praying together, sharing concerns and prayer requests.

EVE
The Forgiven Mom

The Perfect Planet, Population: Two

Meet Eve, the most misunderstood mother in the Bible.

She talked to a snake. She had no mom, dad, childhood, brothers, sisters, or awkward teen years. She never dated and was married to the only man for her.

This isn't that makes her misunderstood, though. Eve lived in total harmony with God. The Creator of the world, the omniscient, perfect King of kings was in the Garden of Eden with her. Life for her was, literally, perfect.

So different from our lives today! But you don't need me to tell you that. You know our perception is so foggy, we can't begin to comprehend total harmony with God. Instead, we expect that every day, something will go wrong. We know we'll get sick and, one day, die. Our husband and children and all other loved ones will die, some tragically. And before they die? Each of them will let us down somehow. In our life this side of the garden, we know conflict, death, sadness, and brokenness— not perfection.

I can't imagine Eve's life in the garden. In her day-in, day-out perfect relationship with God, she knew no stress, hate, or discord. Adam never worked late. Eve never nagged him about communicating better or thinking of her needs. Divorce or infidelity didn't exist. She never wondered where God was; He was there in the garden with her. He was available for walks and talks. Eve never fretted over wrinkles or worried about cellulite. She never had to utter those awful four words to Adam ("Do I look fat?") or wonder whether he still found her attractive. She was never lonely or bitter or frustrated. She was never even hormonal.

And then it all changed.

With one bite of fruit.

Eve lost her perfect relationship with God (Genesis 3:8), her ideal marriage (v. 12), and her beautiful home (v. 24). Because of her sin, this future mother, who had never even been aware of the concept of evil (v. 22), would have one son murder the other. (In such a situation, we modern moms would wonder, "What did I do to raise such evil children? Was this my fault somehow? Why, God?")

But Eve? We can never know the depth of the guilt she must have felt upon realizing that she had, in fact, done the very thing that brought evil into the world, the one thing God had told her not to do. While she must have been desperate for forgiveness, I doubt that even she could comprehend the full magnitude of her sin.

Know-It-All

It bothers me that we start our study together with sin, death, and the power of the devil. But the sad truth is that every woman's story begins with the fact that we all mess up in a million different ways, and because of that, we, like Eve, are in desperate need of forgiveness.

1. a. Read Genesis 2:15–17.

   What did God warn Adam about the tree of knowledge?

   b. Read Genesis 3.

   What did the serpent convince Eve to do?

   c. Read verse 6 again.

   Why did Eve eat from the tree of knowledge?

It's inconceivable, isn't it? War, infanticide, genocide, murder, rape, plague, and death—all because one woman broke one rule. One simple rule. One little bite.

Unfair. The consequences don't fit the crime. If God is a loving God, how could He do this to His children? How could He punish billions of people just because Eve wanted to be like Him? But it was more than that. Eve didn't just take a bite of fruit or pass it on to Adam.

2. Reread verse 5. What does the serpent promise Eve, enticing her to break God's one rule?

Eve wanted to know good and evil *independent* of God. She wanted to decide for herself what was good and what was evil. I'm chagrined to say it, but this is where I understand her a little more. Before Eve bit that fruit, she was in harmony with God. Yes, God had created her with the power to choose, but she had lived only in complete harmony with Him. God is good all the time, so her bite was not simply a violation of one small rule; her bite separated herself from Him, from His goodness.

3. Read verse 7 again. What immediately happened after Adam and Eve were separated from God?

4. In your own words, what does it mean to be independent of God? Discuss this with your group or write your answer here.

5. Here's one truth you and I can be completely sure of— life without God is never good. Read verses 16–21. What was God's specific punishment for Eve?

After Eve separated herself from God, everything changed for her. Genesis points out two curses specifically. First, her unique blessings as a woman—pregnancy and childbirth—would now be full of pain. Second, her relationship with Adam would forever be tainted with sin. No matter how compatible, how in love they were, they could never again live as harmoniously as they did before they separated themselves from God.

Perhaps it's by God's grace that Eve couldn't comprehend the far-reaching effects of her sin. At that moment, with the serpent whispering in her ear and temptation in her hand, she would have had no clue how much contractions would hurt. She couldn't know that thousands of years later, a woman would rather have a needle stuck in her spine than endure the full pain of childbirth. Eve couldn't imagine how much she would suffer when she fought with Adam. Or that one day, wives and husbands would know divorce attorneys and child support and parents who never saw their own children.

Satan knew the enormity of her sin. And of course God knew. And He knew something else: Eve, His first daughter, was hurting. At that moment, He made a promise to His guilty daughter, a promise that changes everything forever.

6. Read verse 15. Who is the "He" who will crush the serpent?

As Eve stood in the garden embarrassed by her nakedness, confused by her strange new feelings, angry with herself, furious at the serpent, and guilty with grief roiling in her tummy, she must have been grasping for *something*. Was she desperate for a connection back to God? some clarity about what would happen now? God's words, spoken to the serpent, were the beginning of this clarity. God said Eve would have offspring, and her offspring would crush the serpent. *Kids?* God was giving her children? And one of them would not only punish the serpent, but He would also be stronger than the evil one's lies?

The name *Eve* means "mother to all." As women today, Eve's daughters, we live with this icky inheritance: sin. We can relate to sinful Eve. We, too, have felt confusion and the despair of guilt; we have felt fury with ourselves and were quick to blame others; we have known temptation and separation from God.

God's promise to Eve, the promise of His Son, is our hope today too. If you've felt separated from God, worthless as a mother, or inadequate as a wife, you need only to look to Eve. She messed up *everything*, and yet God brought her back to Him.

Sister, nothing is too big for God! Eve had a personal relationship with her Creator, yet she disobeyed the one rule He gave her. In doing so, she betrayed Him. Did He give up on her? Did He leave her to suffer? Did He turn away from her and leave her to wallow in her pit of guilt? No, He didn't. God's grace knows no bounds. At the very moment He confronted Eve with her sin, He had already provided for all of His children by giving us forgiveness, peace, and perfect love through His Son. Eve's comfort that day in the garden is also our comfort today.

Pray

Heavenly Father, You are more gracious than I can ever understand. Thank You for loving me, even when I betray You. Help me to live in love, trust, and Your grace every single day. In Your Son's name I pray. Amen.

The Mother Sin

Eve was the first woman to experience the sins we know all too well today—anger, guilt, insecurity, and fear. She must have also known the sin that is the mother of the rest: lack of faith. If you're like me, you would rather worry all night than trust God. You would rather grab at the shabby security that money offers than trust the One who can provide everything. You would rather take on the emotional burden yourself than put it on Jesus.

Eve knew firsthand how powerful God was—that He created everything and could just as easily take it away. But could she trust He was also loving? Could she trust that God had forgiven her for ruining His creation?

7. Read Genesis 4:1. What language does Eve use that indicates she understands God's forgiveness?

Eve gives credit to God for the birth of her son. The name *Cain* means "gotten." Eve names her baby with a word that indicates her relationship to God, a name that will remind her that she did nothing to deserve a child, yet God had given her one.

Although Eve had violated her relationship with her Creator, she seemed to know that God had reconciled their relationship. Through the promise of the Redeemer, she is, again, His child. He is her Lord and Provider. She knows He gives her all good things.

8. Read Romans 5:18–21. Eve's sin condemned all people to death. What abounds even more than death?

At the heart of Eve's story is her relationship with God. He created their relationship to be perfect; she disobeyed Him in a quest for independence from Him; her sin broke their relationship; God promised her that He would send a repair for it.

Sister, at the heart of *your* story is your relationship with God. If you're separated from God, if you're frightened and bitter, you are not living in the harmony of forgiveness Christ provides. It isn't God who wants to be independent from you. If you're like me, you forget to pray; you sometimes trust luck over the Lord; you might feel jealous, insecure, petty, and dissatisfied. If you're like me, you are constantly distracted by your "realities" and forget who God is. He is love. He is peace. He is joy and hope. With the help of the Holy Spirit, we see that we live every day in His goodness and mercy. Because God loves us, He sent His Son so we can live in His forgiveness and enjoy a relationship that is truly life changing, truly perfect, truly permanent.

The First Dysfunctional Family

Eve, former resident of Paradise, was about to endure sin and pain deeper than I hope any one of us has ever known.

9. Read Genesis 4:8.

   What horrible grief did Eve see as a mother?

Her firstborn, her baby, murdered her only other child. I can't imagine the pain of losing a child or knowing my son is a murderer, let alone the burden brought on when both of these tragedies happen in a split second. Incomprehensible. If we grieve when our children fight (and that's just normal sibling rivalry), then who can blame Eve for being absolutely heartbroken at the sins of her children? Did she blame God for letting this happen? Did she think back to that pivotal day in the garden and see this event in the context of her own life-altering action? Did she ask God for forgiveness? Did she grasp the enormity of His forgiveness?

10. Eve's story continues in verse 25. Here we have another hint of what she might have been thinking. When Eve is blessed with another child, to whom does she give credit?

Eve still identifies herself as God's child. To me, verse 25 is proof that Eve remains in a relationship with God. This, dear women of God, is evidence of the power of God's grace. Even when we see the destruction we've caused, even when we are in pain, God is still *good.* He still gives us proof of His grace in our lives. We can still count our blessings as gifts from a good and gracious provider.

In all things—our most tragic pain, our scariest moments—God wants us to turn to Him, to repent. We can do that with the help of the Holy Spirit. God will strengthen us. Through faith, we can see God's goodness in our life, even when everything else points otherwise.

Reconciled

11. In verse 26, Eve gives birth to another son, Seth.
    Read Luke 3:38. What special honor does God give Seth?

God blessed His daughter Eve even after she defiled His creation and was banished from the garden. He forgave her. He reconciled her to Himself. He blessed her son with the Son who offers eternal life. Through Jesus, our Redeemer, God reconciles us to Himself too. That's not just theology—that's day-to-day joy. The sinful world we live in doesn't have to crush us. Sin is not the last word; God's grace is. If you're a mother who has ever looked into the big, sad eyes of a sorrowful little one, you already know this. Your heart melts, and you are moved to forgive your child. God our Father wants to forgive us too. He wants to bring us close to Him again and again through a new relationship with Him—a relationship filled with forgiveness that comes as a blessing of being His baptized child.

12. Read God's words in Isaiah 1:18.

What does He compare our sins to?

13. What about His forgiveness?

To be forgiven in Christ means to move on, not to another sin, but as a new creation. It means that to God, we're pure and clean. Because He looks at us through the lens of His beloved Son, the Creator of heaven and earth sees us as perfect. This is life-changing news, sisters! God separates us from our sin farther than our human minds can comprehend (Psalm 103:12). He did it for Eve. He does it for us when we go to Him for forgiveness—after we scream at our kids, shut out our husbands, hate our co-workers, and gossip about our friends. Because of what Jesus did for us on the cross, when we repent and ask for God's forgiveness, we're free from that ugly sin.

14. Read the renewing words of Acts 3:19–20.

What happens when we repent? What does God do with our sin? How do we feel?

15. In Matthew 11:28, Jesus promises to give rest to those who are burdened. What are your burdens? What rest do you find in His forgiveness? Talk about your answers with your group, or write them here.

Sister, you know the sins that dominate your life. You know what baggage you are holding on to in your heart. God knows those sins too. Confess your sins, turn away from them, ask Him to forgive you, and know the change of living a redeemed life. Just as He did for His daughter Eve, He gives you rest in His peace.

Pray

Father, I hurt You when I sin.
I hurt the people I love. I hurt myself.
Thank You for giving me forgiveness
through Your Son. Help me to live
as Your redeemed daughter. In Your
Son's name I pray. Amen.

Forgiven to Be Forgiving

I believe that many women are sensitive and can easily be hurt. At least, that's how I am. My feelings get hurt so often, I sometimes feel like I'm a walking target. I'm a walking, talking, huge, red-and-white circle to my husband and kids, friends and neighbors, co-workers and, well, almost everyone. (But let me be honest: I'm not just a victim; I can dish out what I can't take.) So many women live their entire lives deserving an apology from someone about something.

Forgiving is hard; that's why so many of us have trouble doing it. I don't know about you, but I'm never quite ready to say I've been hurt or to admit that I'm wrong. It's much easier to nurse my pride and hold on to my pain than it is to forgive or be forgiven. Perhaps this is because true forgiveness, the kind we give in Christian relationships, is so powerful. It's so much easier to ignore it than it is to deal with it.

16. Read Ephesians 4:32. What does God say about how we should handle forgiveness?

When God forgives us, we enjoy a renewed relationship with Him. We rest in His peace, in the right relationship with our Creator. This is truly an awesome blessing—which is why God *commands* us to forgive one another. Admitting you're wrong, saying you're sorry, and truly forgiving another person renews your relationship with that person. God wants His people to enjoy these fresh relationships, just like He wants us to enjoy a restored relationship with Him.

Let me go one step further. There is someone specific waiting for your forgiveness. There is someone specific waiting for your confession and apology. A friend is hurting because you have not forgiven her. A loved one is hurting because you won't apologize to him. Your relationships are a mess, and you're holding on to pain and pride rather than receiving God-given forgiveness and sharing it in kind.

If you feel comfortable, share with your group a relationship in need of forgiveness, or you can write your answer here.

God Loves the Forgiven Mom

What does it mean to be forgiven? "Forgiven" is an identity that changes all aspects of our lives. Because we're forgiven, we have the same hope that our sister Eve felt after she committed the first sin—the sin that turned her life upside down—and after she received God's promise of reconciliation.

Because we're forgiven in Christ Jesus, we have the freedom and power to forgive. As difficult as forgiving sometimes is, can you imagine what life would be like if we couldn't forgive? There would be no chance to mend relationships, no opportunity to move on; there would be no peace or joy or hope. To be forgiven means we can stop seeing ourselves as hopeless victims and as broken criminals. Through forgiveness, God accepts us. Without turning back or dredging up the past, He offers us a clean slate. Through the washing and renewal we received when we were baptized, He makes us pure. Now, that's a message to start with!

17. Forgiveness changes everything. Read 2 Corinthians 5:17. After we've been forgiven, what does God call us?

Sister, this is the message of hope in each mother's story. We may have inherited our sin from Eve, but we also received God's covenant of reconciliation through His Son. That Good News makes us His new creation, living totally in His perfect love.

Pray

Father, thank You for Your grace. (I so don't deserve it.) By Your grace, I have hope. Help me to admit when I'm wrong and to forgive those who have wronged me. Help me to live as Your forgiven, redeemed child, trusting in You. In Your Son's name I pray. Amen.

SARAH
The Insecure Mom

It Takes One to Know One

Let me guess. You've never thought of Sarah, princess of the Old Testament, shining example of submissiveness and faith, model wife and believer, to be insecure. Maybe Hagar, her maidservant, was insecure. (From what we read in Genesis 16, Hagar acts that way in almost every situation she's in.)

But not Sarah.

However, doesn't this point of view depend on the definition of insecurity we use? To me, insecurity means doubt about self-worth. I have decades of real-life examples where my insecurity monster rears its ugly head. This happens most often when there's something I think I need, when my desire for that *thing*—a mate, a baby, a job, a house—pricks little holes in my soul. That desire is a liar. It tells me that I would be happier with the better job. I could be a better mother if I only had a bigger house. The only thing between me and the woman I want to be is these last five pounds. Before I know it, I'm convinced that I'm not whole without this thing. I'm not fulfilled. In a word, not secure. Wait—that's two words. In a word, insecure.

If I were to write an autobiography, the chapters about the insecure times in my life would also be stories about the times I did some pretty stupid things. When I don't feel whole, when I don't feel secure, I try to control everything around me. I try to control the other people in my life. I just *try too hard* at everything. Maybe your autobiography would be different. Maybe insecurity doesn't grip you like it does me. Maybe you're fulfilled, content with what you have. Maybe you float from one season of your life to the next with the ease I'm looking for.

Maybe you're not being honest. Or maybe you're not sure what insecurity looks like. Do you want to look into the mirror of insecurity and see if your reflection is staring back at you? Let's see. Do you become a control freak when you're worried about something? Do you put too much pressure on the people around you, making them responsible for your happiness? Are you self-conscious? self-centered? overprepared in everything you do? Have you ever sent an e-mail that took hours to write when the recipient probably took seconds to read it? Do you seem to worry about your relationships with an intensity that borders on unhealthy? Do you always seem to be looking for the next thing—better *these* or losing *that* or getting through all of *this*—that will complete you?

Changing your circumstances—getting the husband, the baby, the body, the house, the contract—will not fulfill you. There is only one change that can give you true security, sister. Remember your inheritance from Eve. God promises you that He will provide for you. He will give you true hope through His Word and true security through a relationship with His Son, Jesus.

There are so many times I behave as if I'd like to forget that. I would much rather try to control my life, to find my self-worth through something I can buy, beg, or steal.

Meet Sarah, whom I call the insecure mom. How can I say that? It takes one to know one. Even with a specific promise from God, Sarah didn't find her security in Him. Because she was insecure, she tried to control her life, and that proved to be a disaster. She seemed to have it all—the husband, the looks, the money. Everything, of course, except a baby.

Abraham's Right-Hand Woman

Sarah's story begins in Genesis 11, when her name was still Sarai (which means "princess"). Later in Genesis, after Abram participated in the covenant of circumcision and his relationship with God changed, God changed his name to Abraham (17:5). This was also when God gave Abraham the specific promise that Sarah would give birth to Isaac. When He made this promise, He changed her name to Sarah, *"My* princess," to show that Sarah was also His.

For Sarah, insecurity started at home in her very own tent, the one she and Abraham packed up for a trip away from home.

1. Read Genesis 11:29–12:3. What is our introduction to Sarah? What promise did God make to Abraham?

2. Sarah was at least sixty-five years old and probably postmenopausal when she left Ur. Read Genesis 11:30 again. Think about what God was promising to do. Why would descendants for Abraham mean a miracle?

When Sarah traveled with Abraham from Ur, she said good-bye to her family and friends so she could accompany her husband as he responded to his calling from God. But she must have been wondering just how the Lord would bless them with descendants, *millions* of descendants, from her old, dried-up uterus. He had promised to create His kingdom out of *nothing*.

The Lord also told Abraham that he would be blessed to be a blessing. Can you imagine the excitement Sarah and Abraham must have felt, setting off for this life-changing mission trip? God had called Abraham with specific plans and a specific blessing. Today, we see the fruit of that blessing: Sarah's descendants include the Israelites, the great patriarchs (and matriarchs) of faith, powerful kings, and Jesus Christ, Savior of the world (Romans 4:16–25). And through the water and Word of Baptism, you and I are adopted into this great family of faith.

Wow. What a lineage! And what an honor for Sarah, whom God calls honored above women. But where we're meeting Sarah in this study, at the beginning of her story, she had no idea what God had in store for her.

Mother to No One

It's ironic, isn't it? Sarah, whom God eventually calls a mother of nations (17:16), was infertile—and would be for about ninety years of her life. Her son (promised later) wouldn't come for decades. In the meantime, Sarah was Abraham's companion on the faith journey they would tell their grandkids about. But the pinpricks of insecurity must have already begun to poke holes in her happiness even before they were called to go to Canaan. She would someday have descendants more numerous than the stars (Genesis 15:5), but at first, she couldn't get pregnant with even one.

Those very early years must have been torturous. Every menstrual cycle, Sarah would have been focused on—obsessed with—whether or not God would answer her most fervent prayer: for a child, a son. As she kneaded dough for bread, trudged along next to Abraham, or hiked with the other women to fetch water, she must have worried about pregnancy. I'll bet she analyzed every craving, wondered about every mood swing, hoped over every ounce she gained or abdominal twinge she felt. Were these signs of pregnancy? Was God finally growing a baby —*her* very own child—in her womb?

But, no. Despite all her hoping and praying, it wasn't happening. Over and over, God replaced her monthly question mark with a monthly—well, you know.

Sarah, the Rich, Beautiful, Graceful Princess

Just to show that insecurity knows no bounds, let's consider just how gifted Sarah was. God had given her intellect, grace, riches, and a strong will. We learn in Genesis 12:15 that Sarah was so beautiful, foreign kings desired her. When Abraham and Sarah traveled to Egypt to escape a famine, Abraham worried that the pharaoh would kill him to have Sarah.

3. Read Genesis 12:10–20. When Abraham lies that Sarah is only his sister, he places her in great danger; he betrays her to save himself. How does she handle herself in this story?

Sarah is graceful under pressure and loving to Abraham despite his betrayal. We certainly don't see here the trying-too-hard, insecure woman she will become one day, do we? But Sarah still has more than twenty years of infertility ahead of her, plenty of time to become completely obsessed about what her body was *not* doing.

I wonder how this experience in Egypt affected Sarah. Abraham, known for his faith, doesn't display that faith in this situation. Instead of trusting that God would protect them, Abraham lied, selling Sarah out.

4. How do you think this affected her insecurity—both in her faith in God and her faith in her husband? Discuss your answers with your group or write them here.

5. God took care of Abraham and Sarah and even made sure that their sojourn in Egypt was lucrative. His care didn't end there. Read Genesis 14:10–16. Besides the riches that Pharaoh gave them, what other riches do Abraham and Sarah receive (v. 16)?

6. According to verse 14, there were 318 men in Abraham's tribe. When the men went to fight in Sodom and Gomorrah,

they had to leave their families behind. Sarah served as the tribe's temporary leader. What does this tell you about her intellect and her abilities?

Behind Every Great Man

God continued to add to Abraham's tribe in number, power, and wealth. Sarah served as a kind of first lady. Her husband wasn't appointed to be the leader of the free world, of course—his job was even more important because he was uniquely called by God in a personal way. The Lord not only gave Abraham tremendous earthly responsibility, He also increased Abraham's faith.

7. Read Genesis 15. During this covenant, Abraham experiences wonderful, personal promises from God. Abraham surely told Sarah everything that God had promised him in verse 18. How do you think this take-charge woman felt after hearing the Lord's plans for them?

We can certainly feel Sarah's predicament. And her pain. God had given her so much—grace, money, beauty, talent, intelligence, a strong marriage—and now He promised even more! Except, of course, the "even more" of children wasn't happening. Now read Genesis 16:1–2. Maybe you can sense Sarah's restlessness through the text. The couple had already lost valuable time while Abraham was off at war. It looked as though she would never get pregnant. And if there's any place that the weed of insecurity can find fertile ground, it's in fear.

Sarah needed a baby to fulfill God's promise. She was about seventy-five years old by now and well past menopause. Lot, Abraham's only possible heir, was also gone. Didn't God understand that thousands of descendants had to begin somewhere?

Desperate Times, Desperate Woman

I completely sympathize with Sarah's desperation. I would have told myself the same things: "No one has ever wanted a child this badly. No one has ever been infertile this long. No one needs a family like I do."

8. Of course, in Sarah's case, that all may have been true. But when insecurity grabs hold of us, we ignore the most important part of our decision-making process: what God has promised us. Sarah knew God's command. Read Genesis 2:24. What instructions did God give His people about marriage?

32

Sarah ignored this law and focused on what she needed: a baby.

9. Read Genesis 16. When Sarah became insecure, she tried to control her situation herself. She insisted Hagar, her maidservant, sleep with Abraham. Whom did this hurt? How?

10. Sarah clearly betrayed God's law by insisting her husband have sex with another woman. Read Genesis 17:1–21. God didn't respond with anger or punishment. He was gracious and loving. He changed Sarah's name and made what specific promise concerning her (v. 19)?

Happiness Sometimes, Holiness Always

So, Sarah's plan for a baby wasn't turning out very well for her. Instead of the child she longed for, she now faced competition from Abraham's second wife. Instead of the happy family she plotted for, she now had Ishmael,

Hagar's son, living at her family campsite and serving as a constant reminder of her own failure.

Sarah, faithful matriarch of the Old Testament, is starting to look as insecure as a group of seventh graders in the hallway. Like each of us when we find ourselves feeling miserable and unfulfilled, Sarah needed someone to blame.

No matter what your dilemma is, you know how insecurity works; you know how the self-talk goes. Why am I unhappy? It must be my husband's fault. He's too weak; he doesn't understand what I need. Why am I frustrated? It must be her fault; just look at how she treats me. Why do I still not have a baby? That's God's fault; He doesn't understand that it's all about me and what I want. Right. Now.

Laughter

Read Genesis 21:1–7. Finally! A baby! *Her* baby! Sarah's joy in verse 7 is obvious. Have you ever had one of these moments: when you see—really see—the blessings in your life and marvel at how good and gracious God is to you? How perfect His order is? When Sarah was completely focused on her own plan of having a child (her trying-too-hard phase), she discounted God's power. Never did she think God would give a woman as old as herself, a woman in menopause, a baby she would be able to hold and nurse and love. And yet, He provided, just as He said He would.

God called Sarah for a specific purpose, and He provided what she needed for that purpose. God has called you too. Has He called you to be a mother? a supportive spouse? a witness to His love through your profession? God will provide for you too, dear sister. Through His Word, He will fortify your faith. Through the Sacraments, He will come to you to strengthen your relationship with Him. Consider your life—how has God worked despite your insecurity? How do you respond with joy? Share your answers with your group or write them here.

Sarah, Mother of Multitudes

Read Genesis 23:1–2; 24:67. Sarah's story ends happily, doesn't it? Not only did God bless her with a husband who loved her, but also with a devoted son and as many descendants as there are stars in the sky. The miracle of her child's conception lives today through her story. One of Isaac's sons was Jacob, and from his family came the twelve tribes of Israel and, generations later, Jesus Christ.

More biblical space is given to Sarah than any other woman in the Bible. She is named as a hero of faith (Hebrews 11). In her story, we can see how God worked through the life of this strong-willed princess. God wants us to know His promises are for us—He will bless us to be a blessing (Genesis 12:2). God wants to spend time with us through His Word and through prayer and through worship. He wants to repair our souls, which have been perforated with insecurity. Ask the Holy Spirit to work in your life so you can see God's power, love, and grace.

A Promise and a Path

The Lord knows what you need, dear sister, and it is for you. Remember His promise to Eve in Genesis 3:15? He promised the Savior, whose death and resurrection reconciled His children to Himself. Through your Baptism, you are His. Because God is always perfect and always faithful, you can be sure that He fulfills the promises He makes to you in His Word. Because God is who He is, He doesn't make promises He can't keep.

11. Read 2 Corinthians 1:20.

What does Paul remind us about God's promises?

God loves each and every one of us. Isn't that amazing? He gave His Son specifically for *you*. Read Jeremiah 29:11. What plans does God have for you? How is He calling you to share His Word with the world? Discuss your response with your group or write it here.

Waiting Patiently on the Lord

12. Take a step back and think about Sarah, the insecure mom.
    God did fulfill His promise of a child to her.
    Why do you think He waited to do so?

When we see barrenness in the Bible, in women like Hannah and Elizabeth, for example, we see how God works through their infertility. When Sarah, a ninety-year-old woman, gave birth to Isaac, you can bet that people noticed. Certainly, this was no typical child. As news of his miraculous birth spread to the neighboring, idolatrous countries, people would have asked, "Who is this woman's God?" Fertility gods were all the rage in 2067 BC, so anyone who had heard about Sarah and Abraham's powerful God would want to know more. They would recognize that this couple and their descendants were followers of a very special God. *The* God.

In the same way, God gave elderly Elizabeth her son, John the Baptizer. News of his birth spread all over the hill country of Judea. God used Elizabeth's unexpected fertility to send the message that this man was special. We know that as an adult, he taught about someone even more special: Jesus, the Son of God.

If things are out of our control, we can let go of them. Therefore, we don't have to feel insecure about this life or the next because we are not in control. God is. And Bible stories like the one about Sarah assure us that He will work His perfect plan through us, His daughters through Christ.

Despite all of God's amazing promises to us, He never promises us that trusting in Him will be easy. What thing are you waiting for, dear sister? Are you so focused on receiving that thing that you've lost perspective? Have you reached the all-about-me tunnel vision that cuts God out of your life?

When we are tired of waiting for God, He reminds us that we may not understand His timing (Psalm 90:42). Are you struggling with infertility? restlessness in your marriage? feelings of incompetence as a mom? Even as you struggle, you can be confident that God loves you and will give His best for you. You are His daughter, the child of the most powerful King, who will provide for you in His holy and perfect way and time. Sarah is proof of that.

The waiting can still be hard, can't it? When it is, ask God to strengthen your faith. Ask Him to help you understand His plan. Trust that the Lord will provide for you. We can pray, knowing our Lord hears us and will provide for us. God encourages us to trust in Him instead of in our own plans (Proverbs 3:5). God knows it takes courage to wait for Him, courage He will provide (Psalm 27:14).

God Loves the Insecure Mom

In Genesis 18:13–14, God asks, "Is anything too hard for the LORD?" The answer is no. Through His Son, He gives us riches that we could never imagine. In John 11:25-26, Jesus said, "I am the resurrection and the life. Whoever believes in Me, though he die, yet shall he live, and everyone who lives and believes in Me shall never die. Do you believe this?"

Do you believe this, my friend? Do you trust that your heavenly Father has provided for you? Do you trust that He will continue to provide? Do you believe that He can do the impossible (and He will, if it's part of His holy plan)?

Pray

Thank You, Lord, for keeping Your promises to me as you have to Your daughters throughout time. Continue to bless me with faith to trust what I cannot see. Let me love You, basking in the confidence that You are my heavenly Father. Take away my insecurity, Lord, and bless me with the security I have in You. In the holy name of Your Son, Jesus, I pray. Amen.

HAGAR
The Picked-On Mom

An Embarrassing T-Shirt

I recently spent a few minutes people watching at the airport. Isn't the airport the absolute best spot for doing that? I saw so much love that day: a family surprising a daddy coming home from a business trip, a group of foreign exchange students meeting their host families, a gaggle of girlfriends back from a trip to Costa Rica, a grandma mobbed by six ecstatic grandchildren. Seeing such candid love, shyness, and excitement was like having a front-row seat to a reality show. I was smiling and living vicariously through all those emotions.

Until the reality show became awkward. A young girl walked past with a defeated look on her face. She was heavyset and had a large butterfly tattooed on her ankle. But it was her shirt that was awkward. It read "Diamond in the Rough." The T-shirt was faded and too tight, like she had worn it for years. She didn't look up from her flip-flops as she walked past. I cringed for her. Why was she so sad? And what was with her shirt? Was she trying to announce that she was a diamond in the rough? Who prints that message on a shirt? A diamond in the rough is something that's discovered, not announced. Didn't she know her T-shirt made her look desperate?

No one else seemed to notice her as she shuffled past. I watched her file out the airport doors, alone. Who was she flying to see? Was her shirt a message for that person? Was she hoping they would notice her this time? Did she care if she looked desperate to him or her?

And while I'm on the subject, aren't we all desperate? Maybe this girl was actually brave—brave enough to announce who she wanted to be, how she wanted others to see her. Maybe we don't print those words on our T-shirts, but isn't our desire the same? *Get to know me. Please, discover who I am. Appreciate me—the* real *me.*

Have you ever felt that not many people get to know the real you? They may know your identities: mom, wife, teacher, neighbor, volunteer. But these labels can make you—the real you—feel invisible. Who really knows you? Who knows about your desires, hidden talents, fears?

Maybe your family or your lifelong friends know the

real you. A good boss might take the time to appreciate you. But isn't it the sad truth that most people probably won't? To these people, who know only your labels or by what you can provide for them, the real you remains undiscovered.

In Genesis, we meet Hagar, a living, breathing example of someone whom no one saw, whom no one appreciated. Maybe she was a diamond in the rough, but she was also a servant in a foreign land. She wasn't a person who anyone wasted their time with.

She is our picked-on mom.

The Invisible Foreigner

Hagar was an Egyptian servant traveling with Abraham's clan of Hebrews, who were originally from Ur, far away from Egypt. Society was hierarchical in 2067 BC, so a person's status—or level—within the community was important. Their status determined what rights they had and how they were treated. When Sarah and Abraham picked up Hagar on their travels and adopted her as a servant, they took away her rights as a person. If there are any people in history who know how it feels to be invisible, they are servants. They're treated as property, not people.

Not only did Sarah and Abraham have the right to treat Hagar as property, but she was also strange to them. She looked different from the Hebrews. She was Egyptian. Forget the beauty of women like Cleopatra; Hagar's mistress Sarah was the one who stood out in this crowd (Genesis 12:14).

Maybe you, too, have felt prejudice as you've moved to a new part of the country, a new city, or even just to a new neighborhood. The people you meet form an opinion about you based on your accent or your car or your clothes. In the tight-knit group of Abraham's nomadic tribe, Hagar was way different. And different—a foreigner—in the midst of neighboring people who were suspicious and violent—was not good.

1. Think about poor Hagar. How do you think she felt
   to be taken into this clan as a servant?
   Discuss your answers with your group or write them here.

The Invisible Slave

2. Read Genesis 16:1–6. What evidence do we see that
   Abraham and Sarah treated Hagar as less than a person,
   like she was invisible?

3. When Sarah demanded that Hagar have sex with Abraham,
   he was eighty-five years old. Hagar was young, probably
   in her twenties. How do you think she felt about this?

For us, sex between an octogenarian and a young woman has a certain amount of ick factor, but attitudes about sex were different in this culture. Sex was to procreate. Marriage contracts of the time show this. If a wife didn't give her husband an heir in two years, he could take a second wife. Although this was the law of the land, Abraham and Sarah followed Yahweh.

4. Read Genesis 2:24 as a reminder.
   What was God's command for marriage?

But Sarah ignored God's command and insisted that Hagar have sex with Abraham. This made Hagar Abraham's second wife. Becoming a wife to Abraham, the wealthy leader of at least three hundred families (Genesis 14:14), increased Hagar's status within the tribe.

5. How might Hagar, the foreign slave, have felt to be pregnant with the child of such a powerful leader?

6. Read Genesis 16:4. Imagine you're this young slave girl, pregnant with the child of the most powerful man you know. Finally, you're important. Finally, you'll be appreciated— you've been able to do what your mistress could not.

Because your husband is powerful, you are too, right?
People will see the *real* you and realize you're a diamond
in the rough. How did Hagar respond to this blessing
from God, this baby?

7. a. Read verse 5. Did Sarah discover a new appreciation
      for her slave? How did she react to Hagar's haughtiness?

   b. Hagar was now the mother of Abraham's unborn child.
      Did he appreciate her now? Read verse 6. What did
      he give Sarah permission to do?

   c. When Sarah "dealt harshly" (v. 6) with Hagar, we can
      guess that she was probably physically abusive. How
      did Hagar respond to Sarah's abuse?

Fleeing for Freedom

Generations and generations later, my heart goes out to Hagar. Yes, she had a bad attitude—God gave her a gift, the blessing of a child, and she used it against Sarah—but I wonder if any of us would have reacted better. After all, you may be in a relationship where you feel invisible, but nothing like this: where your uterus is someone else's, your life belongs to a foreigner who abuses you, and your master neglects you. Hagar "fled" (v. 6), and I'll bet you I would have too. According to verse 8, she didn't have a destination. She wasn't running toward anywhere; she was simply running away.

When life becomes unbearable, when we feel invisible to everyone and abused by some, we all want to flee. Maybe you run to the mall to charge blindly, or maybe you flee to the comfort you find in chocolate or wine. Or maybe you call a girlfriend you count on to take your side. (She's probably your most negative friend, the expert at complaining.) Or maybe you don't run anywhere. Maybe you choose to take it on the chin, to stay and suffer in silence.

Hagar fled to the desert. And at this place and time, this was the equivalent to suicide. If the wild animals didn't kill her, traveling bands of thieves would. Or the heat would. If she hadn't brought food or water, she would soon die of dehydration. That's exactly what was happening to Hagar—she was hot, hopeless, and probably dehydrated—when the angel of the Lord came to her.

8. Read Genesis 16:7–10. The angel of the Lord (actually the Lord Himself) provided for her. What did He give her?

Promises, Promises

The Lord called Hagar by name. Hagar must have felt so special, so important. The Lord didn't stop there. Besides water, He also provided instruction and encouragement. God gave Hagar the promise of whom her unborn child would be, which was exactly what this miserable and brokenhearted servant girl needed.

Read Genesis 16:11–16. The Lord continued to provide for Hagar. A mom who has had an ultrasound knows the thrill, the promise, of finding out about the baby she's carrying. The Lord's words in verse 11 was a similar thrill for Hagar. First, the Lord announces that she is pregnant—something Hagar would probably have been worried about after her trek through the brutal desert. Then the Lord promises that she would bear a son. Hagar would be successful—she would make it through childbirth (quite an accomplishment in 2067 BC)—and the baby would be a boy! This would be Abraham's firstborn son. This is the first time the Bible records God naming a child before birth. Hagar's baby would be called Ishmael, which means "God hears." God had heard Hagar's afflicted cry; He was with her where she was; He answered her.

9. List the ways Hagar experienced God's grace
   in the middle of the desert.

10. To us, the next part of the Lord's promise might sound
    like a threat. If you're mother to a son, you may know the
    struggles of trying to tame "a wild donkey of a man" (v. 12).
    But how do you think Hagar, an oppressed slave, felt about
    this news—that her child would be free and a fighter?

11. a. What does Hagar call the Lord (v. 13)?

    b. What does this name mean to a woman like Hagar,
       a woman who has been invisible to everyone?

What's Love Got to Do with It?

What strikes me the hardest about Hagar's story is
God's amazing love. Today, we live in a culture where love
surrounds us, not just between families at the airport,
but also in open, overt expressions between parents and
children, husbands and wives, friends and neighbors.

It's woven into who we are: we *love* our jobs; we *love* our friends; we *love* pedicures; we *love* chocolate chip cookie dough.

Not the case in 2000 BC. A woman's goal was not to be loved, but to survive! People, especially nomadic clans like Abraham's, lived close to nature. Famines, animals, and vicious traders could attack at any time, wiping out an entire community. These threats seeped into every part of daily life. A woman didn't have the luxury of falling in love and then getting married. She didn't have the time to ponder what made her happy or what she loved. Hagar, a servant in a hierarchal society, definitely wouldn't have had the time, energy, or even desire to wonder what she loved or who loved her.

And there was surely no love from the pagan gods that almost everyone in Egypt worshiped. Pagan religions were not two-way relationships; their gods did not love. They were concrete objects that were worshiped. Yet this Egyptian civilization believed that these gods were capricious and cruel, and those who followed such deities believed that only extravagant offerings could please them.

As Hagar learns through her meetings with the Lord, this God is different. He treats her with love; He provides for her, encourages her. His love to this lowly servant surprises even me, a twenty-first-century Christian woman, and I've known my whole life that God is love. But this love, so rare in Hagar's culture, is truly amazing. Truly gracious! How special the Lord must have been to Hagar, who likely didn't consider love as a possibility in her life.

What about your life? Where do you see God's love?

Discuss your answer with your group or write it here.

El Roi

Our Lord is El Roi, the God of seeing. He sees *everything,* certainly our sins. He is holy and perfect, so our sin is against His very nature. But He also sees us for who we are: our strengths, desires, and hurts. God knows us intimately because He is our Creator, and He loves us with the perfect love of a holy God. As our heavenly Father, He is compassionate. He is the God who saw an Egyptian slave woman in the desert and provided her with water, encouragement, and promises. And He is the God who sees us in the desert of our sin and provides us with the life-giving water of Baptism, the encouragement of the Holy Spirit, and the promises of His Word. Thank the holy and perfect Father, who sees us and loves us as His children.

12. Read 2 Corinthians 1:9. How do we feel as sinners? What is our hope?

Child of God

13. In Genesis 16:9, the Lord tells Hagar to go back to Sarah.
Why do you think He would command this?

When Hagar ran away from Sarah, she retaliated against her mistress in the only way she could: she took Abraham's heir. Although Sarah was abusive and Hagar was desperate—running away because of her desperation—God intended that Ishmael live with and learn from his father, Abraham. Over the next thirteen years, Abraham was able to teach Ishmael how to make a living and how to live in the Lord. He also circumcised Ishmael (17:23), an important covenant that marked him as one of God's people.

14. How do you think Sarah and Hagar got along after she returned to the campsite?

The Rest of the Story

Read Genesis 21:1–21 for the rest of Hagar and Ishmael's story. Thirteen years have passed since the last time Hagar was lost in the desert and close to death.

15. What has happened in those years?

Sarah insisted that Hagar sleep with Abraham to conceive and bear an heir. But that plan didn't turn out as she expected. Conflict erupted between the women. Living with Hagar and Ishmael was more than Sarah could handle, even after God gave her Isaac, her own child.

16. Why do you think Sarah reacted so strongly to Ishmael's teasing?

The Lord tells Abraham again and again that it would be Isaac, Sarah's son, whom He would bless with a holy lineage (17:16). Read verse 20.

17. What promise does God make about Ishmael?

We don't know what Sarah's relationship with Ishmael was, but it's obvious by her attitude in Genesis 21:10 that Sarah considered him to be a threat to her son, Isaac. Read verse 11.

18. How did Abraham feel about sending off his son Ishmael?

Dying in the Desert

The relationship between Sarah and Hagar doesn't seem to have improved. Sarah still doesn't call Hagar by her name and she doesn't seem to care much about Hagar's feelings—or her life. She wants to make sure that Hagar, the person, remains invisible to her. Sarah sends Hagar and Ishmael back to the desert to die.

In verse 15, we see Hagar, perhaps the first single mother in the Bible, failing miserably. God has given her a child and promised he would be the first of many descendants, and she's letting him die. Hagar has given up. Her anguish is so great that she can't even bring herself be close to her son as he takes his last breaths (v. 16). In her desperation, does she call on the Lord? Does she have the confidence that He will again meet her where she is and provide for her?

No. It's Ishmael, Abraham's son, who has spent the last thirteen years receiving instruction about the Lord from his father, who prays (v. 17).

19. a. What's the first question the Lord asks Hagar?

b. What instruction does the Lord give her (v. 18)?

c. God not only gives Hagar instructions and a plan,
but what does He also show her (v. 19)?

Our Nearsighted Problem

Our God is the God who sees. His perfect vision shows how nearsighted we are. Like Hagar, who didn't see the well of water, there are times when we can't see beyond ourselves. When we're miserable, we don't pray to Him. When we're confused, we forget to look to His Word for instruction. When we're thirsty, we don't turn to His sacramental meal for refreshment that can truly quench our soul's thirst.

Discuss the following questions with your group, or write your answers here.

20. a. Think back on your day, your week, your month. When have you felt invisible?

b. Where did you turn?

c. What did you receive: temporary help or a real change of heart?

d. After reading about God's grace to Hagar, how can you grow closer to the God who sees?

Diamond in the Rough

God, the one who sees, loves you. He wants you to see Him too, and He wants to provide you with love and hope that can truly change you. He wants to meet you where you are and show you His grace. He wants you to understand His promises of forgiveness and salvation that are available through the death of His Son, Jesus. You are His "diamond in the rough," whom He is shaping to reflect Christ.

God Loves the Picked-On Mom

Sister in Christ, God provides for you. Every day. He clothes you and gives you a place to live, friends, and family. But He provides for you in so many more significant and life-changing ways. He gives you His Word, filled with comfort and encouragement, and He promises that reading it will transform you. He gives you the gift of Holy Baptism, in which He made you His own daughter and an heir to eternal life in His kingdom. And He gives you Holy Communion, the very body and blood of His Son to forgive you and sustain you.

How do you respond to God's grace when you feel invisible and picked-on, when you feel like you need to get away? Do you flee to His promises, to His Word?

If you're like me—and I think you are—you do turn to the Lord. But not always. Even when we know those promises are there, we're tempted to first choose to flee from that food He provides and to our favorite department store or restaurant or gripe session. El Roi, the God who sees, patiently invites us to come to Him and trust that He will look through the lens of our Redeemer to see us for who we are. He will meet us right in the desert and give us exactly the water of life that we need.

Pray

God, You see me, even with all my faults, sins, and selfishness. Because of Jesus, You see me as forgiven and redeemed, and You love me. Thank You, Lord, for providing Your life-giving Word and Sacraments to me. Help me to understand Your love so I can seek You out. In Your Son's holy name I pray. Amen.

REBEKAH
The Skeptical Mom

Older, Wiser?

Whoever said that youth is wasted on the young must have been saying specifically that youthful **skin** is wasted on the young. Wait, youthful skin and hummingbird metabolism are wasted on the young. Oh, and bottomless energy. Because if I would have known then what I know now about what eventually sags, withers, and slows wayyyy down, I would've appreciated all the nights I ate chocolate cupcakes for dinner.

Women in the second half of life are trying to undo the damage we did to ourselves in the first half. Back when we had dewy skin and shiny hair and the energy to stay up late eating sweet desserts, we didn't realize how much money we would one day spend exfoliating and moisturizing and dieting. Walk through any shopping mall in the country, and you'll see the billion-dollar industry of beauty products that promise the collagen and elasticity we took for granted in our youth.

At least when we get older, we also get wiser. What a relief, right? Who would voluntarily go back to their torrid adolescent years? Well, maybe for those cupcakes, but only if we could take some of this hard-earned wisdom with us. Amen? But it isn't just wisdom (and wrinkles) we get with age. There's something else: cynicism, skepticism, a hesitancy to trust with the wide-eyed gullibility we had way back when. Maybe that's exactly what wisdom is—experience plus skepticism.

Meet Rebekah. When we're first introduced to her in Genesis, she's youth personified. She's beautiful, energetic, and eager to trust. But as we follow her through her long life, she loses much of that. Actually, I'm not sure if she loses her beauty. And even in her old age, she's pretty energetic. But she certainly loses her eagerness to trust.

Specifically to trust God.

As you read her story, think about your own ability to trust. Walking with God means having faith that He loves you and will provide for whatever you need. Do you believe that? If not, you may also be a skeptical mom. And you might learn a lot from Rebekah.

Wanted: One Strong Woman

When we last left Sarah and Abraham, they were
cuddling their long-awaited miracle baby, Isaac.

1. a. Read Genesis 23:1–2. What has happened in Abraham's life?

   b. Read Genesis 15:5. What promise had God given Abraham?

   c. Read Genesis 24:1–4. What needs to happen next so
      the line of Abraham can continue?

   d. What concern does Abraham's servant have?

   e. Read verses 10–14. Abraham's servant is clearly
      nervous that he won't find the right bride for Isaac.
      What does he do?

Read verses 15–28. And ladies, here she is. Rebekah enters the scene in dramatic timing that can only be divine. And she's beautiful! And hospitable! And energetic! And look, she's even watering the camels. Praise the Lord—before the servant could even finish praying, Rebekah steps up as an answer from God.

Have you experienced God's dramatic timing? Have you asked Him for something that seemed to happen instantly, miraculously? Talk about this or write your answer here.

Maybe you, like Abraham's servant, had a specific problem. Isaac needed a strong wife—literally strong in the physical sense. (After all, this woman would be the mother of generations; she couldn't be old or weak.) Abraham had already stressed that Isaac's bride had to come from his own clan in Paddan-aram. The servant needed the right woman to appear. And behold, a young woman with enough energy to water ten camels came. The well was probably a spring that was accessible by steps. If each camel drank thirty gallons, she would have to run up and down those steep steps about eighty times.

Carrying huge clay pots of water.

Wow.

The servant must have watched this future mother of generations with a smile on his face.

Praise and Thanksgiving

2. Read verses 22–25. What further information does the servant find out about Rebekah that proves she's the right girl for Isaac?

3. What does the servant do in verses 26–27?

What a wonderful example for believers throughout the generations. Not only does the servant ask God for specific help, but even in the excitement of finding Rebekah, he also stops to thank God for His love and faithfulness. When God answers your prayers, do you thank Him? Do you see the blessings in your life as those things divinely provided for you by God? Talk about how you thank God, or write about it here.

REBEKAH • THE SKEPTICAL MOM

It can be challenging to see everything we have as gifts from God, especially when those gifts come in the form of what we don't have. After all, even the biggest scoffers in the world, those who publicly claim that God doesn't exist, enjoy nice houses, plenty to eat, and supportive families. Aren't blessings for believers? How can a nonbeliever have more than we do?

4. Read Philippians 4:19. What does God promise Christians?

God provides blessings, including Jesus Christ, to every single person, His entire creation. Those without faith don't see these things as blessings. They deny Jesus Christ and don't thank God for what He has provided for them.

5. God gives His blessings out of grace, not because they're anything we deserve. Read 1 Chronicles 16:34–35. What's our response to these free gifts?

Take a few minutes right now to thank God for the blessings He has put in your life. You can say the prayer that follows or your own prayer.

Pray

Heavenly Father, Your love is different; it lasts forever; it's perfect. Thank You for Your love and Your care. Thank You for everything You give me: my life, my family, and my friends. Thank You for the food You give me and for my home. Most of all, Lord, thank You for Your Son, my Redeemer and Savior. In His holy name I pray. Amen.

Love at First Sight

There was one more crucial quality Rebecca needed so she could be the mother of Isaac's babies: faith. Not only did she have to come from a godly family, but she also had to be a believer herself.

6. Read Genesis 24:50–61.

What evidence do we have of her faith?

Rebekah had it all: enthusiastic hospitality, boundless energy, family connections, youthful beauty, and strong faith. She was truly a gift from God for Isaac. Let's all enjoy the moment when he sees that for the first time.

7. Read Genesis 24:62–67. Ah, a marriage made in heaven. Based on what you know about the culture in 2000 BC, what's significant about Isaac and Rebekah's marriage?

In a culture when marriage was first about procreation, it's unusual to read about a husband who loves his wife. But we can relax in the knowledge that Isaac loved Rebekah for the rest of his life. He was faithful to her too.

Prayers and Answers

Rebekah and Isaac's happy family runs into problems when they fail to produce the family part. For about twenty years, Isaac's wife was barren, just like his mother had been.

8. Consider Isaac's conception, famous for its miracle. What do you think he'd heard about it?

9. a. Read Genesis 25:21. Isaac is desperate for a child to continue his family line with the descendants God had promised to his father, Abraham. What does he do?

b. How does God answer Isaac's prayer?

Read verses 22–26. Rebekah felt the children struggling inside her. She was worried about her pregnancy.
Did this mean a miscarriage? If she was able to carry the
twins, would she have a catastrophic delivery?

10. Read verse 22 again. Where does Rebekah turn for answers?

For the third time in Rebekah's story, we see the power of prayer. Abraham's servant prayed, and his prayer
was answered before he could even say "Amen." Isaac
prayed, and Rebekah conceived twins. Rebekah prayed,
and God answered her prayer directly!

If you've prayed fervently before, then you know that
the act of prayer changes you. Focusing on God puts Him
where He should be in our lives—right in the center. We
see Him as vast as He is, as omniscient, as our Creator
who knows us better than anyone else; we trust Him as
our heavenly Father. This happened to Rebekah when she
asked God about her pregnancy. She believed He could
explain it to her. She believed God would provide answers.
And He did. There is no hint here of the skeptical mom
she would later become. Instead, she looks to God and
trusts Him because she knows exactly who He is.

REBEKAH • THE SKEPTICAL MOM

How do you see God? Do you see Him as the Creator, powerful enough to form all the earth out of nothing? as Jesus the Redeemer, loving enough to forgive all your sins? as the Spirit, who gives you faith? Talk about your answer, or write it here.

The One Mom Loves Best

Perhaps the next part of the story is where Rebekah becomes a skeptic. Or maybe this is just when she makes a tragic parenting error that generations of mothers have been guilty of. She chooses a favorite child: Jacob.

11. Read verses 23–26 again. Which child is born first?

Rebekah never forgot the information God had given her. Contrary to the ancient custom, her older son (by just a foot) would serve her younger son. Neither Jacob nor Esau deserved God's favor, but God chose to give it to Jacob.

Rebekah must have often thought of God's promise as her sons grew up, but she didn't trust it—Rebekah took matters into her own hands.

12. Read verse 28. Rebekah's parenting problem began with one word: *but*. What dysfunctional family politics are in Rebekah's family?

Notice the text doesn't say Isaac loved Esau *and* Rebekah loved Jacob. It's clear from the "but" that Rebekah's love ran deep and only to Jacob.

Read on. We'll see more about how this favoritism played out for the skeptical mom.

The Older, Wiser Skeptic

13. Although Rebekah started out with so much promise, although she had the love and commitment of her husband, her life was not easy. Read Genesis 26. What trials did she have?

14. How do you think each of these events led Rebekah to lose her faith in God?

During these years in Gerar, Rebekah's life was hard. She survived the scary experience of starvation during the famine. She mourned Esau's choice to marry nonbelievers. She stood by as her husband lied that she was his sister. Perhaps all these events led to her loss of faith, which we'll see in the next part of her story. But before we go there, consider this: where do you turn when your life is hard? Think back to a tragic time in your life. Did you rely on God? Talk about your answer with your group or write about it here.

The Why over the How

Besides remembering God's promise, I can imagine another reason Rebekah loved Jacob best. Jacob might have seemed like the child more suitable for God's favor.

15. We see Esau's impetuous, shallow personality in Genesis 25:29–34. What does he do that shows these characteristics?

If this episode between brothers shows that Esau makes hasty, silly decisions, it also shows that Jacob is contemplative and scheming. Characteristics they'll be remembered for over thousands of generations. And now we see Rebekah in her full glory as the skeptical mom. She never forgot that the Lord would bless Jacob, but she did forget one part of her conversation with God: *He* will provide answers.

When it comes time for Isaac to grant his blessing, an older, cynical Rebekah doesn't trust that Jacob will receive it without her help. Does she ask God for guidance? Does she remember that God is powerful enough to do anything and, certainly enough to carry out His promise to bless Jacob? Does she lean on God to guide her as she had as a younger believer?

16. Read Genesis 27:1–40.
   What does Rebekah do instead of trusting God?

Rebekah was skeptical of what God could do and would do. She traded the comfort of resting on God's promise for action. Surely, Rebekah had also told Isaac about God's promise to bless Jacob. If Isaac knew about God's plan, he was in direct defiance of God's will by blessing Esau instead of Jacob.

17. Do you think this was Rebekah's motivation to scheme against her husband? If so, does this excuse her actions?

God in My Pocket

Have you also been guilty of "helping" God—or not even acknowledging Him? Think about your last big decision. Did you see God as your loving Creator who provides you with blessings, answers, and guidance? Did you pray as an afterthought? Or did you pray at all? The bad news is that we may be guilty of the worst of these sins. I know I am. I might as well carry God in my pocket like a lucky rabbit's foot for as small as I sometimes make Him. I can go entire days without talking to God, although, deep down, I know His power and His desire that I pray.

But the good news is that God still loves me. He still wants me, His daughter, to come to Him with all my questions and my worries—and my thanksgiving. God also wanted Rebekah to trust Him, to ask Him how to handle the situation of Isaac's blessing, to share her worries with Him.

But she was skeptical.

And she didn't.

Older, Wiser, Bitter

For all of Rebekah's early promise, life doesn't end so well for her. Her tragic mistake of tricking her husband had consequences more far reaching than she could have imagined.

18. Read Genesis 27:41. What does Esau, the quick-tempered hunter, decide to do?

19. Read verses 42–46. What solution does Rebekah have to save Jacob?

Rebekah knew that Esau was erratic and spontaneous. She sent Jacob to her brother, knowing Esau would eventually calm down and her favorite son would be able to return.

20. Read Genesis 31:41. How many years is Jacob with Laban?

I think it's sad that Rebekah lived her final years separated from her favorite son and died before Jacob returned. When Isaac and Esau discovered that Rebekah had schemed against them, they would have been disappointed and hurt. Rebekah's skepticism caused her and those close to her a great deal of pain. She's a good example of how growing older doesn't necessarily mean we're wiser.

God Loves the Skeptical Mom

I'm going to be honest with you—I think that one of the reasons most of us don't pray fervently is because God doesn't seem real to us. Of course, deep down, we know there's a God. But we're too busy. Life is too jam-packed with problems that need our time and energy to think much about an abstract idea like God. Our culture encourages self-reliance. Trusting in a God who ruled thousands of years ago seems irresponsible. Besides, God helps those who help themselves, right? Doesn't the Bible say that?

Well, no, actually. That's not in the Bible, which makes me sad because I'm so good at trusting myself. And I would be better at trusting God if He were more real—if only He would talk directly to me. That would make it easier to trust Him.

Except, of course, it wouldn't. I mean, look at Rebekah. God *did* speak directly to her, and she still lost faith. Maybe one reason God included her story in the Bible is so we would see that the problem is not with how He interacts with us; the problem is with how we respond to Him.

We listen to scientists who claim God doesn't exist. We listen to pop culture that tells us God doesn't matter and we can achieve happiness on our own. We listen to media that promises peace is just a nicer car away.

21. If this sounds like you, read Romans 1:18–23.

Here Paul addresses those who don't believe in God.

Read verse 20. How has God shown Himself to us?

22. What does Paul warn against in verse 21?

23. Read 1 John 4:7–9. What evidence do we have of God in our everyday lives?

24. Read John 3:16. What further proof do we have that God loves us and wants to have a close relationship with us forever?

25. Read Matthew 18:2–4.
    What kind of faith does Jesus tell us to have?

Big questions. And God doesn't want us to struggle with these questions on our own. Once we're led to see who we are and who God is, our skepticism is diminished. Studying God's Word provides many more answers on who He is. And like we've talked about, prayer keeps us focused on Him as our true center and not on ourselves.

Worshiping with other Christians fortifies our faith through relationships with others as we lift each other up. Hearing the Gospel proclaimed in the sermon and receiving the Lord's Supper puts us in Christ's presence. And when we're there, we can be certain we're not alone.

Pray

Heavenly Father, give me Your Holy Spirit to infuse my life with faith. Let me see You through Your creation, through Your love for me in Jesus, and throughout my life as Your beloved daughter. Lead me to You in all parts of my life. I trust that You will provide for me for Jesus' sake. Amen.

JOCHEBED
The Faithful Mom

Bad Guys

The other night, my three-year-old son couldn't get to sleep. They had discussed stranger danger at school that day, and his usually secure world was turned upside down. His fears went something like this.

Mommy, did you know there are bad guys who want to steal our stuff? Bad guys with big guns and masks." Leave it to a little boy to turn strangers into the villains he sees everywhere from cereal boxes to movie posters.

I told him not to worry; we lock the doors at night.

"So, there *are* bad guys?"

I had used the wrong tactic.

"Bad guys who will come into our house while I'm asleep?"

I had no answer, because, of course, there are bad guys who might come into our house while we're asleep. Together, we said a prayer that Jesus would keep our family safe.

He wasn't done. My kids have advanced degrees in bedtime stalling, and he wasn't going to let me out of his room that easily. "If they broke into our house, what would they take?"

"They won't break into our house. But if they did, they would try to take our valuables."

He spotted another line of questioning. "What are our valuables?"

I had to think. "Well, like . . ." Our cell phones? No, they were old and barely functioning and sold for a dime a dozen at a kiosk in the mall. Our computers? Hardly. Also old. Mine has been acting like a stubborn diva who takes a nap whenever I ask her to save or open a document. Stealing her would do me a favor. Our TV? The bad guys probably have televisions nicer than ours. "Maybe my wedding ring."

Sam jumped out of bed. "They would take your wedding ring off your finger while you were asleep? They would steal your finger?" He marched over to grab my hand. "They would take *you*?"

Again, wrong tactic. But I knew the answer for a silent night of sleep was around here somewhere; I was just missing it. "You know what, Sam? I don't think we have anything a bad guy would want. Our stuff just isn't that valuable."

"Nothing? What do they steal from other peoples' houses?"

I turned out the light. "They take really nice jewelry or expensive things that families have had for years, so they become really valuable." I kissed him for the fiftieth time since my original command that it was time to go to bed.

He finally climbed under the covers. "And we don't have any of that kind of stuff?"

"Nope." I saw my escape, and I was taking it. "We don't have anything like that at all."

Sad, but true. Other families may have heirlooms—rare book collections or antique jewelry or paintings worth thousands of dollars—but not us. This idea bothered me for the next few days. Our house is filled with lots and lots of stuff—cheap toys, on-sale clothes, disposable appliances—but nothing of monetary value. No heirlooms. I had been honest with my son; we had nothing worth stealing, nothing that couldn't be easily replaced. Did other families have valuables they were saving for the next generation? Or do we all live in such a disposable society that we have more trinkets from the dollar store than anything really worth keeping or stealing?

The Heirloom of Faith

I wrestled with these questions for a couple of days before I saw the delightful truth. There was something our parents had passed down to us that we would pass down to our kids—*are* passing down to our kids. Our faith traditions. Through mealtime prayers, weekly worship, discussions about the Sunday School lessons, bedtime Bible stories, and impromptu talks about Jesus, we give our children something more precious than anything that would sell at an antique shop. We are giving them the tools of faith, teaching them the life-changing truth of Christ's Gospel, and reinforcing for them the hope that can be theirs for the rest of their lives.

My husband and I don't always do a good job at this. Many nights, I fall asleep mid-prayer, asking God to help me be a better example of Christ's love to my kids. There are times when we don't have daily devotions or talk about the Sunday School lesson. But I know the kids notice that we take our worries to the Lord in prayer and we thank Him when the storms have passed. They know that Sundays are for church and Saturday nights are for small-group Bible study. As they learn more about the bad guys in this world, I pray they know there are some things even the worst guy in the scariest mask can't take from them.

Not that we have anything else to take. Unless the bad guys want a temperamental computer or bins full of Happy Meal toys.

Rich Mom, Poor Mom

Jochebed was faithful in teaching her children about God. She lived her faith by example. She was poor, and her people, the Israelites, were enslaved by the Egyptians. But she had a rich history of faith, and she shared it with her family.

1. a. Read Exodus 2:1. Moses introduces his mother
   as a "Levite woman." God honored Jochebed's
   tribal family, the Levites, by choosing them to lead
   worship for His people. She was also a granddaughter
   of Jacob and had surely learned about the Lord
   at the knee of her parents and grandparents.
   How was this identity important to her as a believer?

   b. How did belonging to a faithful Hebrew family shape
   who she was as a mother?

   c. God blessed Jochebed in another magnificent way.
   In 1526 BC, children were the greatest blessing
   a person could have. Read Numbers 26:59.
   Who were Jochebed's children?

2. Moses, Aaron, and Miriam would become three of the most famous people in all of history. Moses delivered the Hebrews from Egyptian slavery. Aaron became the founder and center of the Hebrew priesthood, which he served for almost forty years. Miriam became the leader of the Hebrew women. How are these faithful children a credit to Jochebed as a mother?

3. As the descendant of Abraham and Sarah, Jochebed's family history reads like a Who's Who of the Hebrews. God also made her rich by blessing her with children. But she was not rich with wealth. Read Exodus 1:8–22. How was Jochebed poor?

4. The Egyptians worshiped idols and lived in corruption. They despised Yahweh and His people, the Israelites. Besides being poor, what else had the Egyptians taken from Jochebed and her family?

Terrorism and Genocide

Disgusting, but true. The pharaoh was threatened by God's people, and he took away their freedom. He wanted to wipe them out by destroying their sons. When he decided to get rid of them once and for all, he ordered a terrible decree.

5. a. Read Exodus 1:8–22. What was this terrorist's plan for genocide?

b. Read verses 19 and 20. How did the midwives avoid the pharaoh's plan to destroy the Hebrew people?

c. What was Pharaoh's new plan to end the Hebrew people?

Fearless Plan, Dauntless Faith

6. a. Read Exodus 2:2–8. Jochebed shows her quick thinking
   and faith. How did she follow the Egyptian law and
   also trust that God would keep her family safe?

   b. Read Exodus 2:9–10. How did Jochebed's fearless plan
   and faith work out perfectly for her as Moses' mother?

   c. Jochebed nursed Moses, but as his primary caregiver,
   she was able to provide for him with more than just
   her milk. What else do you think she taught him
   in all the hours she spent with her son?

   d. What inheritance did Jochebed give to Moses?
   Describe how she might have done this.

Big Payoff

Jochebed's plan worked perfectly. If you remember your child's infant and toddler years, their favorite person is the one who provides the food. For Moses, that was Jochebed. When she trusted that God would protect her son, God blessed her so she was able to serve as Moses' constant and favorite caregiver. Jochebed nursed and nurtured the son who was supposed to be killed! By the time Moses left his mother to live in the palace as an adopted son to Pharaoh's daughter, he understood his identity as a Hebrew, who his family was, and God's covenant promises.

7. Besides what Jochebed told him,
   how do you think he saw his mother's faith in action?

8. We see Miriam's role in this story also. How does she show her mother's traits of faith and quick thinking?

Imagine what instructions Jochebed may have given Miriam. As a child of the pharaoh's palace, Moses would have access to the best education in the world.

9. How do you think this contributed to God's plan for making Moses a great leader?

Read Hebrews 11:23–28, from the Bible's "Hall of Faith." Moses left Egypt "not being afraid of the anger of the king," just as his parents were "not afraid of the king's edict."

10. How was this family tradition of following God instead of society important to who he became as a man?

Popular Opinion Says

We are tremendously blessed to live in a free society. Most have us have never known real oppression. In fact, we have an almost incomprehensible number of opportunities. By our Constitution, we are guaranteed freedom to practice our religion, raise our families as we want to, live wherever we chose, and openly love the Lord. The terrorist rules of the pharaoh in Exodus 1 are shocking to us.

But how free are we, really? We may not have a dictator commanding us to kill our own children, but we are threatened by something else that can be even more influential: popular opinion. You may be free to love God openly, raise your children the way you want, and practice religion whenever you please, but do you? Society—popular opinion—tells you that you're worshiping an irrelevant God. Best-selling authors announce that Christians cling to faith because they're insecure or unrealistic. Biblical principles are considered old fashioned and even radical by popular opinion. Openly loving God is countercultural. Telling society that God doesn't condone living together, gay marriage, and abortion will get you tagged as closed-minded and intolerant.

11. Jochebed was faithful to God, even when society (Pharaoh) told her to do something else. How well are you doing at saying no to popular society? Give an example of something popular society tells you to do, and describe how you respond.

What about your role as a Christian mother? How have you taught your kids that following God is more important than following popular opinion? Discuss your answers with your group, or write them here.

Read Hebrews 13:7–8. Doesn't this verse capture the story of Jochebed, the faithful mom, perfectly? The writer of Hebrews reminds us that God will preserve our faith for generations. Our children will imitate us. Jesus Christ is the same yesterday, today, and always. What a promise!

12. Read Hebrews 13:6. What does God promise us?

Sister in Christ, I have struggled with this issue more than any other in my spiritual journey. Although I know God's commands and I am certain of His promises, I also know lots of people who ignore what God says or who don't believe it. I don't agree with their beliefs, but I like these people. Nothing is harder than *not* listening to their opinions, especially when they seem so wise. Well, almost nothing. As my children get older, it's even harder to teach them that being a Christian means being different and that loving God means living in light of the Scripture rather than the darkness of public opinion. After all, on television, on the Internet, in school, and in news media, popular opinions rule like little pharaohs, telling us what to do, what to believe, and how to behave. Who can argue with the power of that?

Do As I Say, Not As I Do

13. Can we show our kids the fruit of living in God's promises? We can! Read Deuteronomy 6:5–7.
    What command does God give us?

14. Describe how you "love the LORD your God with all your heart and with your soul and with all your might." How does Moses say we should teach God's commands to our kids?

Teaching our children to love God isn't reserved for Sunday School or weekly worship. It doesn't only happen at devotion time or right before bed. It happens every minute of every day, during all those nothing moments when your kids are watching you.

As you know, kids are excellent imitators. There are times when I don't want to acknowledge how true that is, but when I hear one of my children say something in my exact tone of voice or I see one of them mimic my pose or gesture, I am reminded I have little copycats watching me. It's one of the first rules of motherhood: your kids will do what you do. Your child's teacher can tell which parents practice good manners and who burps at the table without saying "excuse me." Want to teach your kids to be angry? Yell a lot. Want them to be the first to curse on the playground? Use plenty of four-letter words at home. Hoping they'll give you sarcastic retorts? Answer your husband that way.

But if you hope to teach your kids the fruit of the Spirit, treat them with patience and kindness. If you want them to turn to God when they're happy as well as when they're afraid, include them when you pray. If your deepest desire is to give them a rich faith life, let them see you reading the Bible. Allow them to catch you praying with your husband. Call on God's name, but not when someone cuts you off in traffic.

15. Read Galatians 5:22–23.

What is the fruit of the Holy Spirit?

The Next Generation

As far as mothers go, Jochebed isn't a well-known one. Her name is mentioned only a couple of times in the Bible. (The word processor on my temperamental computer keeps underlining her name in red, thinking I must be making a mistake.) But her faith lives on through the faith of her famous offspring. Learning about Jochebed's story is an opportunity you have as a Christian mother to be countercultural, to teach your children about the truth of Jesus Christ and how living in Him can change their lives to be filled with real joy and real hope.

Think about your opportunity, my friend. What would you like to change about your life to include more *examples* of your faith for your kids? What habits would you like to start now? Discuss your answers with your group, or write them here.

Things Unseen

So, Jochebed is made famous through the lives of her kids. But did she know who they became? Did she live long enough to see Aaron lead worship, Miriam become a prophetess, or Moses to raise his arms so her grandchildren could pass through the Red Sea and escape Egyptian oppression? Well, she is a faithful mom, after all, so I'm guessing that she believed God would work through their lives, even if she didn't see it. Isn't that the definition of faith? The "conviction of things not seen" (Hebrews 11:1)?

Scripture doesn't say if Jochebed was still living when Moses left Egypt and fled to the wilderness (Exodus 2:11–15), but when God spoke to him from the burning bush, Moses was eighty. Jochebed had probably already died. She probably never knew all the specific ways that her children remained faithful to God and furthered His kingdom.

Maybe this sounds sad to you, but to me, it's a relief. As a mom, I don't need to know every little detail of my children's lives or how God works in them. I'm trying to be content and trust that He will. Even when I'm not around to witness it, the Holy Spirit is still growing their faith, still leading them to Jesus, their Savior, still keeping them faithful.

What are your deepest hopes for your kids? What do you hope they know about their heavenly Father when you're not with them? Discuss your answers with your group, or write them here.

Take a moment right now to pray for your kids. Pray that the Holy Spirit will direct their faiths to be fruitful to further the kingdom of heaven. If you're not a mom, pray for the next generation of believers. Ask God to work in your life, where you are right now, to witness Jesus Christ to others so you can show them God's love through your faith and actions.

Your Legacy, Their Inheritance

That Jochebed was a descendant of a very important Hebrew family was significant to her identity as a wife and mother. Consider your identity. What part of your history is important to you? Write about it here, or discuss it with your small group.

The inheritance you give your kids includes so much more than material possessions. (Thank You, Lord.) It includes traditions, habits, and beliefs. Perhaps you're a child of immigrants or an immigrant yourself. Do you hope to pass down your native language to your children? Or maybe your legacy includes something else. Would you like to see them attend the same schools you did or pursue the same career you have? What family traditions do you hope your kids continue? What faith traditions do you hope they continue? Write about it here, or discuss it with your small group.

God Loves the Faithful Mom

16. Read 1 Peter 2:9.

Why did God call us into the family of Christ?

Through the death and resurrection of Jesus Christ, you have been called, dear sister, into the family of believers. You are in possession of a gift more wonderful than anything money can buy: eternal life with your heavenly

Father, who created you in love and redeemed you through your Savior. What joy to know we aren't captive to the sin of this world! God calls us to live as His own people, and He gives us His commands to protect us and glorify Him.

God gives you the distinct privilege to share this joy, this identity, with the next generation. Preach it to them with your words, but more important, with your actions. Live the life of a redeemed Christian, listening to your Father's voice rather than the voice of popular society. Trust that your kids will see your example and follow it. Pray that they, too, will live within the plans and grace of their heavenly Father. And what a grace that is— so powerful, even the bad guys can't take it from us!

Pray

Heavenly Father, You have chosen me to be Your daughter. Thank You for the chance to live in Your perfect grace. Forgive me when I don't show Your love to my family. Strengthen me through the Holy Spirit to share Your promises with others. Let me live in the light of Your Word instead of the darkness of this world. In Your Son's powerful name I pray. Amen.

RUTH
The Blended-Family Mom

It's Who You Know

A few years ago, my husband quit his job.

He had worked as a consultant for years and put in his time crisscrossing the country as he worked with his clients' projects. Then we had three little ones, and he was ready to tuck them into bed in person rather than sing lullabies over the phone from a hotel room a thousand miles away.

His intentions were good, but it was still a scary situation for all of us. He gave himself one month to land the perfect new position: the job should pay what he's worth, it should be challenging, and it should give him lots of responsibility and room to advance. And most important, it should enable him to be home every night with his family. A pretty tall order, especially in today's job market, but he was determined.

First, he wrote and rewrote (and rewrote) his résumé. Because I'm a writer and actually enjoy wrestling with the twenty-six letters of our language, he enlisted my help. If you've ever fretted over a résumé, I'll commiserate with you. It's grueling, isn't it? How do you make it say "I'm willing to work really hard" without appearing desperate? And then there's the problem of salary. How do you state how much you think you're worth without looking greedy? And when deciding what to include and what to omit in the work experience category, did it seem like he was bragging? Would potential employers recognize his skills from what we could cram into a one-page document?

Once he had a decent résumé, he submitted the thing everywhere. In our paperless society, simply posting his skills on Monster.com put him in on the radar of thousands of employers. Suddenly, he was juggling all these balls in the air (actually, all these résumés in cyberspace). Keeping track of the job openings—what to pray for, what to hope for—kept me awake at night, hoping God would sort it all out for us soon.

Then there were the interviews. And the headhunters. And the networking. It turned out that looking for a job was a full-time job.

There was one bit of advice we kept hearing: if you want a job, tell everyone you know. Past employers, neighbors, family members, church friends, and even former co-workers—anyone who knows you and what you're capable of. Although Mike had a pretty good résumé and he's good at interviewing, there's a lot to be said for people who will, well, say a lot about you. Especially if they say nice things.

It's so true. It's not what you know; it's who you know.

Mike did land his ideal job, one that met every hope on his list. A former colleague had started a consulting company that did only local work, specifically so dads could be at home at night with their families. Another prayer answered, and God did this one through relationships.

The Book of Ruth is all about relationships. In only four chapters, we read about several life-giving relationships: Ruth and her mother-in-law, Naomi; Ruth and her future husband, Boaz; and Ruth and God. As the saying goes, it's who you know. Through the story of Ruth, the blended-family mom, you'll see that God works through every type of family situation to bring us closer to Him.

Let's meet her.

A Bit of (Icky) History

You've heard about Ruth. You might know she was a selfless woman, a believer with an amazing capacity to commit and serve in the name of God. Well, yes. She was all of that. *Eventually.*

Ruth's story is one of growth and redemption. When you consider who she was at the beginning of her life story, you'll see just how far God can take a person. Her history begins darkly. She was born and raised in Moab, a country with an icky backstory.

1. Read Genesis 19:30–38. The Moabites are descendants of what relationship?

See what I mean? Ick. And if you think that's cringe-worthy, there's more. The Moabite civilization worshiped the pagan god Chemosh (1 Kings 11:7). Like other people who worshiped pagan gods, the Moabites believed their god was cruel and impossible to satisfy. So in an attempt to appeal to Chemosh, they worshiped it in the darkest, most disgusting ways. Not only were they pagans, but they freely practiced polygamy and idol worship.

2. Read 2 Kings 3:26–27. What does the king of Moab do to appeal to his civilization's pagan god?

The Moabites were bitter enemies of the Israelites, God's chosen people. Yet, when a famine struck Bethlehem, Elimelech and Naomi took their sons to Moab. During their stay in that pagan country, the sons married local women, Ruth and Orpah.

3. Read Ruth 1:1–5. How long was Naomi's family in Moab?

Discuss with your group how Naomi must have felt when her sons took Moabite wives. Or write your thoughts here.

A Season of Emptiness

If you thought Naomi experienced conflicting emotions when her sons married Moabites, read on.

4. Read Ruth 1:1–18. What extremes of happiness and sadness did Naomi endure during her ten years in Moab?

5. Perhaps the greatest blessing to Naomi was Ruth. In verses 16–18, she made an unforgettable commitment to Naomi. What promises did Ruth make to Naomi?

The words "till death do us part" make us think of wedding vows, but Ruth makes this kind of forever commitment to her mother-in-law. And it's very interesting, isn't it? Ruth doesn't stall, she doesn't ask for anything, she doesn't look back, and she doesn't seem afraid. Clearly, Ruth has faith that the God of Israel, a foreign God to her, will guide and preserve her.

Elimelech, Naomi, and their sons worshiped Yahweh while they lived in pagan Moab. Ruth and Orpah, as part of the family, would have followed the same religious practices. But when Orpah chose to stay in Moab, it means she chose to marry a Moabite and return to her pagan religion. Ruth "clung" (v. 14) to Naomi and vowed that Naomi's God would be her God (v. 16).

6. Read verse 14–15. What is the difference between Orpah and Ruth?

7. a. Put yourself in Ruth's sandals. How was this vow to follow God different than worshiping Him as her husband's God?

   b. How is Ruth's vow like a modern-day confirmation?

Naomi, "Pleasant"

Ten years before, Naomi and Elimelech had left for Moab because they were in a desperate situation. But when Naomi returned to Bethlehem, her circumstances weren't just desperate. They were tragic. She had no money, no food, and no way to get either one. Compounding her situation, she had no husband or sons. Women couldn't own property, so without a male family member to represent her, she could not buy back Elimelech's land.

In verse 20, Naomi said, "call me Mara" (which means bitter). Although Naomi announced that "the Almighty has dealt very bitterly" (v. 20) with her, there were two blessings in her life that she was not seeing.

8. What does Naomi have (v. 22)?

Read Ruth 1:19–22. Can't you just hear Naomi's bitterness through this text? I can. And besides her bitterness and fear, something else strikes me about the way Naomi talked about God in these verses. Despite the fact that she was trudging through the depths of bitterness, she didn't say "There is no God" or "I won't believe in a God who would do this to me." Naomi believed God had "brought [her] back empty." Yes, she was angry and bitter. But did you also hear her acknowledge that God was in charge of her life?

As you'll see through Naomi's story, and as you've seen through your own life, God always loves us and He always provides for us—in His time. When we lose faith because our lives don't unfold exactly as we planned, we sin. Remember how God answers our prayers? He answers with a "yes," a "no," or a "wait, I have something better in store for you."

Share (either with your group or in this space) a time when you felt deep sadness or believed that God had "dealt very bitterly" with you. What blessings came from this sad time?

Any time you feel hopeless about your situation or you wonder why God is allowing you to suffer is a good time to remember your Baptism. Through it, Christ binds you to Him in love and forgiveness. This is an unbreakable binding. You are forever and eternally God's beloved daughter and you can trust that He loves you, wants to be close to you, and works through your circumstances—no matter how bitter or tragic—to bring you close to Him in faith.

Ruth, a Friend

Ruth is described as a Moabite six times in her story, so we know that her national identity is significant. As a convert to Israel, she would have had a lot to learn about the God of love. While she traveled with Naomi, lived with her, and surely prayed with her, Ruth would have learned about the Lord by watching Naomi's personal relationship with Him. What a difference this loving God would have been compared to Chemosh, the capricious pagan deity Ruth had grown up with.

9. a. In Ruth 2:1, Ruth meets Boaz, a "worthy man" who also loves God. What do you learn about Boaz in this chapter?

b. Read verse 12. What blessing does Boaz say to Ruth?

c. Ruth now had relationships with two people who loved the Lord of the Israelites. Both Naomi and Boaz were very kind to her. Through their lives and actions, what message did these believers give Ruth about Yahweh?

Have you heard the phrase "lifestyle evangelism"? This means that actions speak louder than words. Sharing faith by openly loving God and treating the world with kindness is often a very effective means of evangelism.

RUTH • THE BLENDED-FAMILY MOM

Share a time when you've witnessed Jesus Christ to someone through your lifestyle or a time when someone shared Jesus with you through his or her life. Tell your group about it or write about it here.

A Season of Sweating

Since Israelite Law didn't allow women to own land, God provided for the poor and widowed through laws for the needy (Deuteronomy 24:19).

10. a. Read Ruth 2:3. How did Ruth get food for herself and her mother-in-law?

b. Gleaning may have been charity, but let's be clear: gathering barley wasn't easy work.
What do we learn about Ruth in verse 7?

c. As a hard worker, what reward does Ruth earn?

God's law gave specific instructions for how the community should care for the poor. Jesus asks those of us who have much to share with those who have nothing (Luke 14:13). For Ruth, who was young and able to work, this meant providing for her mother-in-law, who was too old to glean in the fields. Although the work was exhausting, we see Ruth joyfully gathering the barley, working for hours in the broiling Middle Eastern sun to get enough food for her mother-in-law. She humbled herself to help someone else.

Think about the blessings God gives you. Maybe you have wealth, time, or a specific talent. How do you use those blessings to bless others? Do you, like Ruth, give cheerfully (2 Corinthians 9:7)?

11. Read Matthew 20:26–28.
    What command does Jesus give us?

Ruth, a Catch

Ruth was young and probably attractive. She certainly could have relied on these features to get ahead in Bethlehem, and who would blame her? She had experienced enough pain at the loss of her husband; didn't she deserve to be taken care of? But Scripture doesn't show Ruth viewing her situation this way. Instead, she invests in her relationships by serving. She takes care of Naomi by working hard for their food. She impresses Boaz with her diligent, physical work. In response to their compliments, she is humble and kind.

12. For generations, women have read Ruth's story
for inspiration. Women have also read Proverbs 31:10–31
for another model of a virtuous woman.
Read that description now. In your own words,
what are some of the characteristics of a virtuous woman?

Which of these characteristics stand out to you as ones you'd like to emulate? Discuss them with your group, or write them here.

A Different Kind of Redeemer

God had provided for Ruth and Naomi's immediate need for food, but they still had long-term concerns about their future. For Naomi, who loved Ruth, this season must have been another difficult one—Ruth was working hard to support them, but she was still young! She should be married; she should have children.

13. God's law provided for widows in another way.
Read Deuteronomy 25:5–9.

What could Ruth do to regain the land of Naomi's family?

Naomi knew that a kinsman-redeemer could provide security for them and a family for Ruth. She also knew that Boaz, who Ruth had already met as her employer, was an honorable and godly man.

14. a. Meet Naomi the matchmaker! What does she encourage Ruth to do in chapter 3?

b. In Ruth 3:10, Boaz tells Ruth that he knows she could have married for love or for money. Why did Ruth choose to marry Boaz rather than a younger, wealthier man?

As the saying goes, it's not what you know; it's who you know. Through her relationships, Ruth now has a husband, a home, and faith in the one true God.

Dear sister, God wants to have a relationship with you, a closer one than you have now. He loves you. He wants you, His creation, to know Him and to know true forgiveness. This is the only way you can find true peace and happiness. God offers all this to you through His Son, Jesus. Boaz redeemed Naomi's land. Can you imagine what a relief that would have been? She wouldn't have to work in the hot sun to pick up stalks from the ground anymore. She had a husband who would protect and provide for her. She had the opportunity to give birth to children of her own!

15. Read Philippians 4:6–7.

    What do we have through Christ, our Redeemer?

A Season of Fullness

16. Read Ruth 4:13–22. Romance writers call this the HEA (happily ever after). List the ways that Ruth's story ends well.

Talk (or write here) about a time in your life that had been filled with blessings. Do you find it easier to trust God when life is going well or when it's hard? Why?

Cheap Clay Jars

Isn't Ruth's story satisfying? I think I enjoy the Book of Ruth so much because I see real people there, real relationships. Naomi is a believer who has an infectious faith. Ruth is a faithful servant who is humble and hardworking. She's unique in her capacity to commit to Naomi and to Boaz. Boaz recognizes his future bride as an honorable woman and—practical man that he is—marries her. We see these same characters in our own lives, don't we? Fallible, fragile humans loved by an infallible, unconquerable God.

17. In 2 Corinthians 4:7, Paul calls believers "treasure in jars of clay, to show the surpassing power belongs to God." What does this mean to you?

Although the people in the Book of Ruth are likable and admirable, their relationships are easily broken. This is also the case with families today, which can disintegrate way too easily. So it's important to remember that our treasure is not our humanness, but our relationship to Jesus Christ. Through Him, we have the real treasure of forgiveness. Through Him, we have the privilege of carrying His message of forgiveness and peace to the world.

God Loves the Blended-Family Mom

Want to know another interesting thing about Ruth's story? Different women see different things in it. There are those who read it and see the message that "family sticks together no matter what." Ruth's commitment to Naomi is testament to this philosophy; these two women are family, so they would cling together forever.

Others point out that Ruth and Naomi were not technically family when she commits to her former mother-in-law. These women read the Book of Ruth and say it's a story of love that doesn't know definition. Women make their own families, whether comprised of beloved friends, neighbors, or co-workers.

Still other women see Ruth's commitment to Naomi as a commitment to another sister believer. When Ruth promises, "your God will be my God," she is proclaiming the bond that sisters in faith have felt for millennia.

I'm aligned with this last group. After Ruth commits to the Lord, Naomi's God, she follows His commands. She shows love and service to Naomi. She marries Boaz, a believer, although she could have married someone younger or wealthier.

No matter what, though, the most important commitment message in this story is God's commitment to us.

18. Read Matthew 12:50.

What family do we have through Christ?

We never see Ruth in action as a mom, but we know who she is by her relationships. Ruth, Naomi, Boaz, and Obed made an unconventional family, didn't they? They may not meet our standards for a traditional family, but they shared a mutual commitment of love for one another and for God.

Our perfect God loves all of us, even those in imperfect families. Like the saying goes, it's who you know. And God wants each of us to know Him through His Word, revealed in printed form and proclaimed from the pulpit. What's more, God knows us! He created us, made us His in the waters of Baptism, and He preserves us through the Holy Supper. It is in this perfect relationship our Lord makes possible that we experience the blessings that last an eternity.

Pray

Thank You, Lord, for the relationships You give me, relationships with people who lead me to You. Thank You for committing to me by sending Your Son. Help me to commit to You through Your Word, through Your Sacraments, and in my prayers. In Jesus' name I pray. Amen.

HANNAH
The Single-Minded Mom

The Myth of the Very Merry Christmas

Every year, I promise I'll be different. I tell myself that **this** is the year I will not devote all of November and December to the perfect Christmas. I will not be consumed with trying to make our life a re-creation of a Thomas Kinkade painting—all of the kids happily wearing matching dress clothes, a cozy candlelight service as snow falls outside, cheerfully-wrapped gifts waiting under a seven-foot Christmas tree and near a roaring fire.

This year, I will keep my expectations in check with reality. For example, we rarely have snow in Texas. My kids aren't thrilled with matching dress clothes. But have I been able to keep my Christmas expectations in check? Not yet. As soon as the first keepsake ornament appears in the window of our local Hallmark store, my promise is forgotten. I'm stung by the perfect-Christmas bug, and my single-minded focus is achieving that vision. For the next two months, my mind is like a sieve, filtering out everything except the million ingredients needed to create the perfect Christmas. My running dialogue is something like this.

Gifts! Teachers and family and the kids and friends and the kids' friends. Homemade cookies and popcorn balls, bargains and splurges, red and green tissue paper and foil bows.

Cards! Coordinating outfits, a picture with everyone looking in the same direction, a thorough (but not braggy) newsletter, one hundred cards featuring a radiant Virgin Mary and peaceful Christ child. Nativity stamps and coordinating envelopes.

Decorations! Thousands of white twinkling lights, real holly and pine-cone wreaths, a tree covered with school-project ornaments, a hand-carved nativity scene and a children's version that plays "Silent Night" when the kids push the star.

Traditions! Christmas choirs, **The Nutcracker Suite**, school plays, caroling, Christmas Day worship service, and hay rides.

Of course, you know the end of this story. The only perfect Christmas was two thousand years ago, and I had no part in planning it. So, no matter how focused I am, my expectations are either too high or misplaced. By Epiphany, I'm absolutely exhausted and more than a little let down. I'm in a funk that lasts clear until spring, when my single-minded focus on the Christmas season is replaced by dreams of the hazy, lazy days of summer.

And come next November? You guessed it. Despite my best intentions, my mind is again preoccupied with creating the Christmas of my dreams. Before I know it, I'm buying tartan taffeta dresses and shopping for coordinating bows. Thomas Kinkade images are, again, dancing in my head.

What Drives You?

I hope that between the two of us, I'm the only one silly enough to spend all of Advent with such a single-minded goal, the only one shallow enough to give up a couple months of my life to live for a myth. Maybe you've never experienced this obsession for a very merry Christmas, but you've probably experienced this focus about something. You know what I mean—when you're so driven that you view every part of your life through that particular lens. Still not sure what I'm talking about? It's like the difference between browsing and buying. When you're browsing at the mall or the grocery store or a yard sale, everything's a possibility; you take time to look and linger and consider. But when you're there to buy, you're on a mission to find what you need. You zero in on specifics and ignore everything else. You focus your energy like a laser beam. You know exactly what you want and you're there to get it.

Have you become obsessed with the myth of the perfect *something*? No? What has driven you? If you're with a small group, discuss something you've been single-minded about, or write it here.

Has there ever been a season in your life when you were completely focused on God? Maybe you were studying His Word. Maybe you were praying fervently for something. How was that focus different? What did it feel like?

Through the course of writing this Bible study, I've spent hours deep in Scripture. My husband teases me because I haven't had a recent conversation without talking about a mother of the Bible. This intense focus on God and His grace has changed me. I'm more loving to my family. I'm more aware of the blessings in my life.

I'm more thankful for who God is and how He provides. I'm more single-minded, and my mind-set is more focused on Him.

I'm more like Hannah, the single-minded mom.

God-Centered Mind-Set

Hannah was one unique woman. She looked at life through the lens of faith. For Hannah, difficulties (and yes, she had many) were an opportunity to trust God. Blessings (lots of those too) were her chance to praise Him. Because of her unique perspective, because of her unique faith, she may remind you of Jochebed or Mary. Like these mothers, Hannah had faith so extraordinary that she was able to take that thing she wanted more than anything else—and then give it to God. Truthfully, that's not just faith; that's faith as the driving force in her life.

We're all driven by something. Do you know someone who's driven by bitterness or guilt? Someone who's driven to please everyone she meets? Someone driven to compete with (and beat) everyone she knows? Your driving force is what gets you out of bed in the morning; it's what influences you as you plan your day and make decisions.

If your community is anything like mine, there are a lot of people who are driven by status and money—what they buy now, when they can afford a bigger house or a nicer car. Others are driven by perfect children (an oxymoron, most moms would agree). Or losing ten pounds. Or climbing the career ladder.

All these people are single-minded about something; Hannah was single-minded about her faith.

Bitter Roots, Flowering Faith

Hannah is intriguing because she is an inspirational example of faithfulness through hardship. The Bible reports nothing negative about her, but she had plenty of negative things going on in her life. To start, she was infertile. We've seen this before. Infertility for women in the twenty-first century is difficult enough; infertility in during this time was considered to be a curse from God, and it opened all kinds of painful doorways. To deal with this situation, Hannah's husband, Elkanah, had another wife: Peninnah. If a polygamist husband wasn't enough, Peninnah was fertile and mean. She teased Hannah because she didn't have a child, which was what Hannah wanted more than anything else. Talk about rubbing salt in her wounds!

1. a. Consider another infertile woman we've gotten to know. Read Genesis 16:1–2. How did Sarah handle her problem of infertility?

   b. Read Genesis 30:1–3. How did Rachel, Sarah's granddaughter-in-law, handle her own infertility?

Read 1 Samuel 1:1–11. Hannah's reaction is intriguing. Instead of fighting back, complaining, or doing what I probably would have done—hide from the polygamist husband, barren uterus, and cruel rival—Hannah worshiped God. She even made a pilgrimage each year with her husband and Peninnah—and Peninnah's kids—to the tabernacle (probably for the Feast of Booths). Seeing the same families with more and more little ones year after year must have been awful for Hannah. She must have prayed desperately for a child of her own, yet her arms remained empty.

Still, Hannah handles her infertility better than other women we've seen so far. Rachel claimed she would die without children, and both Rachel and Sarah tried to take things into their own hands by pushing their servants on their husbands. But Hannah prayed.

2. Read verses 7–8. How do you know that Hannah was deeply sad about her infertility?

Read Jeremiah 29:11. We all have pain in our lives. How do you respond to yours? Do you view your pain through the "woe is me" lens or through the lens of faith, trusting God has a plan—a good plan—for you? Let's go one step further. Have you ever asked yourself the question, "How can I use my pain to serve God?"

Sex and Cheating at the Tabernacle

The annual pilgrimage to the tabernacle would have been painful for Hannah for another reason. During the time of the judges, Eli was the high priest in Shiloh, and his corrupt sons were also serving as priests there. For women of God like Hannah, seeing corruption at the tabernacle—the Israelite center of worship—would have been disheartening.

3. Read 1 Samuel 2:12–17, 22. What sins were Eli's sons guilty of?

4. The tabernacle was built to house the ark of the covenant, the throne for the very presence of God. Why would the corruption of Eli's sons been discouraging for a faithful believer like Hannah?

Worship. Prayer. Learning. Praise. These are some of the most meaningful activities for believers. The Holy Spirit, the very presence of God, is there when we worship Him—whether it's the weekly Divine Service with our congregation or in a convention center filled with thousands of believers.

In the next part of Hannah's story, we see her enjoying time with her heavenly Father in prayer. Little did Hannah know that as she spoke to God so earnestly, her intense prayer would get her into trouble with Eli, the high priest.

Blessing and Belief

Read 1 Samuel 1:12–18. Hannah's prayer was so passionate that it startled Eli. He assumed she was drunk. Given that it was festival time, that Hannah was praying without voicing any words, and the general corruption of the tabernacle, drunkenness wasn't too radical of an accusation.

But Eli didn't know Hannah, our single-minded mom, who was completely focused—completely consumed—by faith in God.

5. What is her response to Eli's accusation that she's drunk?

Poor Hannah. She really can't catch a break, can she? No baby, a mean co-wife, and the priest yelling at her for being drunk.

6. But here's where life starts to turn around for Hannah. Eli recovers quickly from his accusation and recognizes her genuine worship. What blessing does he give her?

7. How did Hannah react to Eli's blessing? What does this tell us about her?

As soon as Eli gave Hannah the blessing, she trusted it. There were more reasons for her to *not* trust this blessing (the tabernacle was corrupt, she had probably asked for a child before, she may have been too old for conception), but she believed she would have a baby. She was single-minded. She didn't see the distractions. Her faith drove her; it was her life lens.

A Vow to God

8. Read 1 Samuel 1:11 again.

What vow did Hannah make to God?

Hannah's vow could have been a Nazirite vow (a person's promise to not cut his hair, touch a dead body, or drink alcohol). Or, by promising to not cut her son's hair, she could have been promising he would be "set apart for the Lord." In Israel, a man without a haircut would have been strange, a mark that he was different.

Read Numbers 30:6–15. When Hannah made this vow, she was not only promising that *her* son would serve God, but she also vowed that Elkanah's son would be set apart for the Lord.

9. According to laws concerning vows,

what does this tell us about Hannah's husband?

Hannah, the Single-Minded Mom

Here, in 1 Samuel 1:21–28, is where we really see Hannah as single-minded. Sure, she had prayed fervently. Yes, she had made a vow to God. But would she follow through? Could she really leave her precious little boy at the corrupt tabernacle with the priest who had scoffed at her? What about when she's snuggling that new baby, nursing him and staring into his inky blue eyes? Would she really be able to keep her promise?

Read verses 27–28 again. Yes, Hannah is the real deal. She is our single-minded mom. She doesn't fear. She isn't bitter. She is so completely devoted to her Lord that even her beloved son, whom she wanted more than anything else, is given over to Him.

10. In verses 21–23, Hannah does not travel to Shiloh for the yearly sacrifice because she is at home nursing Samuel. What does this show us about Hannah?

Besides caring for Samuel by providing physical nourishment, she surely also provided spiritual nourishment, teaching him about God, His covenant, and His love. In these first years before Hannah weaned her son, she must have told Samuel about the vow she had made.

You can bet this would have been a bittersweet time for the two of them. He would be set apart for God, but he would also have to live away from his mother. Hannah must have explained to her son that he was what she had wanted more than anything else, yet she had promised him to God.

What about you? Think about what you want more than anything else. Could you give it back to God? Discuss or write your answer here.

11. Read 2 Corinthians 8:2–5; 9:6–7.

What does God tell us about giving away what we have?

The Faith-Focused Mind-Set

In the movie of Hannah's life, this is the key scene. How will she leave Samuel at the tabernacle? Will she cry out in agony? Will she lecture Eli and his sons about how to treat her darling Samuel? Will she be bitter about losing what she's wanted more than anything? Will she walk away in resigned sadness?

12. Read I Samuel 2:1–11. How does Hannah
    act in the moment of giving her child to God?

Unbelievable! Hannah *rejoices* that she can leave her child in the tabernacle, in the presence of the Lord! Forget the corruption of Eli's sons, never mind her loneliness for her toddler, this single-minded mama sees only God's blessings surrounding her. What an example of faith! Her lens is focused with twenty-twenty accuracy on who God is and what He is doing in her life and in her son's.

13. Read I Samuel 2:1–5. Hannah's mind-set is God-centered
    rather than self-centered. Discuss this statement or write
    your response here.

14. Read I Samuel 2:6–8 and discuss it. Why does our self-
    centered mind-set bring us low? How does God exalt us?

15. Read 1 Samuel 2:9–10 and discuss it.

    By relying on ourselves, we set ourselves up for failure.

    How does God help His followers?

The Fruit of Hannah's Faith

Hannah was single-minded in that she looked at everything through the eyes of faith. She saw that God blessed her as a mother because her son was uniquely called by God. Samuel became a judge and a great prophet; he anointed Saul and David to become kings.

16. Read 1 Samuel 2:18–21. What else did God give Hannah?

17. Read 1 Samuel 2:2–10; Luke 1:46–55.

    What similarities do you see between

    Hannah's song of praise and Mary's Magnificat?

18. Read Galatians 5:16–24. What blessings are ours
    by living a life grounded in God's promise?

God Loves the Single-Minded Mom

19. Read Matthew 16:24–28. Jesus commanded His disciples:
    "Take up [your] cross and follow Me."
    What does this mean?

Read Philippians 3:14–21. Paul urges Christians to "press on toward the goal for the prize of the upward call of God in Christ Jesus. . . . Only let us hold true to what we have attained. . . . Keep your eyes on those who walk according to the example you have."

20. How is this good advice for how to become
    a single-minded mother?

21. Read Romans 8:5–8. Paul reminds believers that when the Holy Spirit lives in us, our minds are filled with "things of the Spirit" (v. 5). What do we have when we're filled with the Holy Spirit?

Are you single-minded, focused on something at the exclusion of everyday life? Think of it this way: What drives you? What helps you make decisions? What motivates your actions each day—the big ones and the small ones? Perhaps your answer is "nothing." Maybe, like me, you're guilty of a different obsession with every season. Have you ever experienced what Paul is writing about in Philippians, how living in the light of God's love—being aware of Him directing your life—is different from the darkness of our temporary desires?

Sister in Christ, this is what God wants for you. As a mother, as His daughter, as His creation, He wants you to see the world through the eyes of faith. He wants the Holy Spirit to drive you. He wants you to live in the love of Christ, your Redeemer.

Pray

Lord, I'm driven by so many wrong things. I let sin be the fuel of my life. Redirect me, heavenly Father. Help me to trust You and see Your blessings in my life. Let me see You in everything. Fill me and my life with Your Spirit. Let me love like Jesus did. In His name I pray. Amen

BATHSHEBA
The Flexible Mom

A Clean Heart

"Create in me a clean heart, O God, and renew a right spirit within me. Cast me not away from your presence, and take not your Holy Spirit from me" (Psalm 51:10–12).

Sound familiar? Maybe you, too, have sung these words during weekly worship. David's plea for forgiveness is part of most church services.

As a mom and manager of a busy household, I can get a little preoccupied with cleanliness. Got a new product that promises to destroy grime or eat up soap scum? I'm the first in line. I'll try anything to erase the tough scuff marks from my walls or the rings from my toilet. (Wow. David's plea for forgiveness makes me think of clean toilets? I guess I am a bit over-the-top.)

Getting a house full of six people clean is difficult enough, but a clean *heart?* Can our hearts ever really be clean? We saw in Session 1 that God sees us as clean not because of anything we do, but because we're baptized and forgiven through Christ. But in the day-to-day dirtiness, that's easy to forget. We're human. We get divorced, we lust after people who aren't our spouses, we yell at each other with the intention of really hurting each other, we let one another down. All the time. We forget to repent and ask for forgiveness. How could any of us hope for a truly clean heart? How could *David* hope for a heart clean enough for God? I've been pretty hurtful to other people, especially those I love the most. (Why do we *do* that?) But David? Ai yi yi. He had sex with Bathsheba who was (oh, whoops!) already married to a noble man of God. When she got pregnant with David's child, he tried to fix the situation by tricking her poor husband. When that didn't work, he just had the guy murdered.

But I'm getting ahead of myself here. The point is that David knew treacherous sin, yet he wrote this very Psalm soon after he had committed these horrific events.

Forget about the spilled-milk grime on the shelves of my refrigerator, David's heart was *dirty*. But he wanted a clean heart, so he poured out his soul to God. He was bold to come before God and ask for His forgiveness and beg Him to make things right again. Although this great king had messed up royally (I know, bad pun), he knew

God would forgive him. David was eager to enjoy God's forgiveness and move on.

Willingness to forgive and forget and move on: that's a description of a flexible mom. Bathsheba was such a mom. What can we learn from Bathsheba and David? Forgive, forget, and stay flexible.

What We Know, What We Don't Know

David was Israel's greatest king, so we know a lot about his life. This shepherd boy was chosen by God for greatness; he defeated Goliath, dodged Saul, fought lots of battles, and brought the people of Israel closer to God. Bathsheba's life, on the other hand, is a bit of a mystery.

1. Read 2 Samuel 11:1–5. What do we learn about her here?

That's why I call Bathsheba the flexible mom. We see in just the first few verses of her story that she went through a lot.

2. Read 2 Samuel 11:6–27. What else happens to her?

With all we know about Bathsheba's life, there's a lot we don't know. She was bathing to purify herself after menstruation, a ritual believers did, but what was her religion? Because her home was close to the castle of the faithful King David, she was probably part of his inner circle. Her father and husband were high-ranking officers in David's military, which gave her some social status. Her husband was a Hittite (who were pagans), but his name was Uriah, which means "My light is the Lord." Bathsheba's husband was a believer, so we can conclude that Bathsheba was too.

Then what about this affair with David? Some read this story and see Bathsheba as a gold-digger, a scheming woman who seduced the powerful and handsome King David to advance herself. Was she? I don't think so. After all, she was bathing in the late afternoon, in the privacy of her home. She wasn't trying to attract attention. Then why did she sleep with him? Let's not forget David was a powerful king. In those days, when the king sent for you, you went.

Because the Bible doesn't give us much about Bathsheba, we don't know about how she dealt with the radical ups and downs that were in her life. Did she turn to God? Did she doubt His mercy?

Absolute Power Corrupts Absolutely

One part of this story that is hard to for twenty-first century readers to grasp is just how powerful King David was. How popular. How *known*. Yes, we live in a celebrity-obsessed society. You can't buy bread and peanut butter for your kids without seeing tabloid pictures of Jennifer

Aniston in her bathing suit and news about how Oprah has more influence than the president. But David had absolute power. The Israelites finally had a king like their rival countries had, and they had made popular King David the ultimate commander-in-chief. His monarchy was a dictatorship—one man, whose wishes were considered unequivocal commands. And as they say, absolute power corrupts absolutely.

The first hint we have that David's power had gone to his head is in the first verse of chapter 11. David's army is out fighting for Israel, but David stays in Jerusalem and seduces the girl next door. Considering this context as a backdrop for Bathsheba's story, you can understand her conflict.

3. Look at chapter 11 again. How else does David enforce his power, and how does this affect Bathsheba?

Bathsheba gets pregnant while her husband was away at war. Because of the timing of her purification bath, those in her household would have been aware of her menstrual cycle. The punishment for adultery was death, so to avoid execution, perhaps she felt she had to cover their sin by marrying David—quickly. David had her husband killed, and Bathsheba was now a widow.

After all the heartache and powerlessness Bathsheba experienced, we can't help but feel sorry for her, can we? David's power and their sin sure wreaked havoc on her life and caused her a lot of pain. Adultery, an unplanned pregnancy, the possibility of a very public execution, and being made a widow by a violent act, and it all started when she was doing the right thing by taking a bath.

Truth and Consequences

Bathsheba had even more pain waiting for her.

Have you heard the saying, "You can choose your sin, but you can't choose its consequences"? God often lets us choose the course of our lives. Although we can chose good or evil, we can never forecast the pain that our sins will inflict on ourselves and others. Sins like adultery and murder may be committed in the heat of the moment, but their consequences last forever.

4. Read 2 Samuel 12:1–15. Nathan shows David
   the truth of the horrendous sins he has committed.
   What punishment does David demand for the rich man
   of Nathan's parable (vv. 5–6)?

Oh, the irony! After he is confronted with his sins, David speaks an oath of punishment—one that God would carry out over the next generation. Four of David's children would die: the baby conceived with Bathsheba in adultery; Amnon, murdered by his brother Absalom; Absalom, who led a revolt against David; Adonijah, who tried to steal the throne from Solomon.

Read 2 Samuel 12:15–23. David pleads with God to save the baby he conceived with Bathsheba, but the child dies. If you could talk to Bathsheba, what would you say to comfort her? Discuss this with your group, or write your answer here.

Perhaps you would remind Bathsheba of God's sovereignty—we can never know the good that God will bring forth from a situation. Or maybe you would give her the same comfort that David speaks in verse 23. He believed that the child was in heaven. God's actions can be a mystery to us—no one understood that more than Bathsheba as she watched her newborn die. Read Romans 8:28. It's true that we can't choose our consequences, but we have this promise from God: for those who love Him, the results are ultimately good.

Talk (or write) about a time that you experienced something terrible, but God used it to His glory.

Read 2 Samuel 12:24–25. Read also 2 Samuel 11:26–27. We read that she married David after he had her husband murdered. The language used to describe this marriage sounds like a publicity stunt, doesn't it? Kind King David marries the widow of his faithful soldier Uriah. If this happened today, the pictures would be splashed all over those supermarket tabloids. Read 2 Samuel 12:24–25 again. The significant part of this passage is that David and Bathsheba conceive another son. The Lord, who works through our pain and tragic circumstances, gave Bathsheba and David a new baby, whom they named Solomon. God sent word with Nathan that the baby was named Jedidiah, which means "beloved of the LORD."

5. How do you think Bathsheba felt about this?

Bathsheba had certainly been through some of the lowest valleys possible, but now, she had to feel the greatest joy to hold a baby that the Lord called "beloved."

I Told You So

You know those reality shows that dominate prime-time and cable television? Even those dramas that showcase raw human pain can't compare with what Bathsheba had gone through in just a short period of time. Adultery with a celebrity (who was a royal), corruption of power, murder, the loss of a child, the loss of one husband and marriage of a new one, and a new baby. Reality show fodder, for sure.

There's something we can learn by reading about David and Bathsheba (or, okay, even from watching reality shows): God gives us His Commandments because He loves us. His Law is there because He wants to protect us from pain and the consequences of sin.

6. Look at the Commandments in Exodus 20:1–17.
   Which of these had David (and Bathsheba) broken so far?

If you looked for it, you'd see each of the Commandments broken on television every night on reality shows, serial dramas, movies, and news reports. And, if you were looking for it, you'd also see why God tells us not to do these things. Sin causes pain. Every. Single. Time.

7. God loves you, dear sister. He wants you to step away from actions that hurt you. Look at the Commandments again. List the possible pain that can come from committing them.

Most of all, the greatest pain comes because each of these sins separates you from the Lord. He created you and wants to be close to you. Breaking these commandments takes your heart away from the gracious God of love. And that will *always* cause the greatest pain.

God tells us over and over that sin hurts us, yet we commit it. And that's why we feel a profound need for

His healing. We want to be back in His presence, just like David did when he wrote about wanting a clean heart.

8. Turn to Psalm 51 and read the introduction.
    When did David write this?

Through David's words, we can feel his pain at sinning against God, the desperation in his confession. Moms certainly know about confession. You warn your children about what will hurt them—from standing on the back of the couch to having sex before they're married—but too often they find out for themselves. And when they do and they're in a world of hurt, they come to you to say they're sorry. As a mom, what do you do? Even if your first reaction is intense anger, love and sympathy follow. When your child is in pain, you want to comfort her; you want to take away his hurt.

9. Read 1 John 2:1–6; Acts 3:19.
    What gift do we have through Jesus Christ?

God's love and absolute forgiveness through His beloved Son allow us to repent and move on. Flexibility is a gift from God that we get through His forgiveness.

Life Source

The opposite of flexible is brittle. A leaf connected to a tree is flexible. It has a life source, so it's supple and pliable. A leaf on the ground is brittle. It's dead and disconnected from its life source.

10. What is our life source as Christians?

11. How are we constantly connected to our refreshing life source?

You may know someone who is consumed by the bitterness of past failures, whose life is dominated by brittleness and brokenness. Or maybe this describes you right now.

Pray

Heavenly Father, You don't want me to be broken or brittle. You provide what I need so I can be flexible, connected to Your life-giving love and forgiveness. Thank You for giving me Your Son, Jesus, so I can stay flexible and connected to You in every part of my life. Amen.

Queen Mother

The drama of Bathsheba's life didn't end with this first episode. Israel was surrounded by bloodthirsty kingdoms. (Israel had become pretty battle scarred.) Throughout the rest of David's torrid reign, he trusted Bathsheba as his partner. This couple with a difficult past moved on to become a royal team. After David died, Bathsheba lived triumphantly as queen mother, the most powerful woman in the country. Her son, Solomon, would grow up to have a wisdom that has been famous throughout history. He presided over a court known for literature, culture, wealth, architectural achievement, and the consolidation of Israel as a nation-state. Bathsheba had to be one proud mama.

12. Read 1 Kings 1:11–31. How was Bathsheba influential in making sure that Solomon reigned as a successful king?

Read Matthew 1:1–6. Bathsheba is listed in the genealogy from the line of Abraham down to David, tracing David's kingly line all the way to Jesus. God worked through the sin in Bathsheba's story to bring her distinction as a believer, a wife, and a mother. It takes a flexible mother to endure the drama that Bathsheba did. And today, her example is offered to us as modern women and mothers.

God Loves the Flexible Mom

My kids are not very good at dealing with change. The first day of any school year has always been like torture. A new home, city, church—they have fought it all. They act like we're out to get them if we even propose a change in their routine.

I don't know if life is ever easy for children, but the ability to adapt sure does help. Adaptability sure helps moms too. The life of a mother is a carnival ride of ups and downs and hairpin curves. If you're not strong enough to bend, you'll break. If you're not connected to your life source, your Lord, you'll crack in your brittleness.

I imagine that Bathsheba had moments when she felt like she was breaking: the deaths of her husband and son, for example. And yet, she moved on and experienced some of God's most radical blessings, seeing her son Solomon reign as a wise king and serving next to him as the queen mother.

13. When we look at the words of Bathsheba's husband David, we can see the secret to her flexibility. Read Psalm 51:10–12. What does God give us that helps us deal with life?

Yes, this is the formula for a flexible mom: a clean heart, just like God originally created us to have; a renewed right spirit through the Holy Spirit; and joy in our salvation through Christ. By forgiving others when they sin against us and by looking to God for forgiveness, God gives each of us the power to move on, the power to confront the sin in our lives. With these qualities, we can handle anything.

Pray right now for God to help you be flexible in Him. Pray Psalm 51, or use the prayer below.

Pray

Heavenly Father, You created me in love. You gave me Your Commandments in love because You love me. My sin hurts You, and God, I'm sorry for my sin. Forgive me for Jesus' sake. Help me know Your love through the Holy Spirit. Help me share Your love with others when they sin against me. And help me move on in love. In Your Son's name I pray. Amen.

ELIZABETH
The Mentoring Mom

Woman's Work

The women of the New Testament would be so surprised to see our lives today. What would they think about the way I sprint through my day? It includes shuttling kids from school to one activity to the next, e-mailing my parents with updates about our family, leaving voice mails for my friends about how much I miss them and how we *need* to get together, and googling recipes with names like "Microwave Magic Chicken" before I finally collapse into bed at the end of the day with a book about how to parent.

It wasn't only that life was slower at the time of Jesus' birth, but also that women's relationships had completely different forms. Families lived together as large clans, with as few as twenty people or as many as a hundred. Women's days were filled with dozens of jobs that the family depended on for their very survival—tasks like weaving, making clothes, gathering water, grinding grain for bread, cooking, and cleaning. While the men left to hunt or fish or work in a profession, the women of the family stayed together to manage the household.

If you have been part of a quilting circle, helped prepare a huge family meal, or organize a fund-raiser, you know what happens when women work together. We talk. We share. We confide. We teach. We learn to trust and to cooperate. This culture of female compatibility was the world in which Elizabeth was raised. She learned the techniques of household management from her mother or grandmother or older sisters or cousins. During long walks to gather water and early mornings making bread, women cared for each other. When a health crisis disrupted the daily routine or a mother was struggling with a child, all of the women shared wisdom and went about solving the problem. Mothering techniques like breast-feeding, swaddling, weaning, or soothing babies were learned from watching other mothers. The idea of looking to a book or some other outside resource to learn how to be a mother would have been confusing to Elizabeth's culture. After all, women had the best parenting experts right at their elbows every hour of every day.

This picture of female support is the backdrop for the next four women we'll study—relationships with other women were not only enjoyable, but also a key to survival.

Elizabeth was into her third trimester when Gabriel told her young cousin Mary that she would give birth to Jesus. Elizabeth was not only able to coach Mary through her first trimester, but she also served as a mentor to the much younger woman. After all, both women were tiptoeing into uncharted territory with unplanned pregnancies that would change the world.

Blessed to Be a Blessing

Ah, Elizabeth. Throughout all the pages of the Bible, it's hard to find a more likable woman of God. When we meet her in Luke's Gospel, she's not yet a mother. And here—you guessed it—are more struggles with infertility. Through Elizabeth's story, we'll see God use her infertility in a miraculous way, a way that shapes the future of the world.

1. Read Luke 1:5–7. Describe Elizabeth's family.

Elizabeth was doubly blessed. Her husband, Zechariah, was a priest. She was also the daughter of a priest in Aaron's family tree. With this lineage and this husband, we know that Elizabeth was a devout believer who tried her hardest to follow God's commands. Elizabeth's family, both her ancestors and her husband, had helped shape her into a model believer.

2. Read Luke 1:7 again. Do you hear a tone of finality in Luke's commentary? Doesn't it sound like Elizabeth had given up on having children? What two reasons does Luke give us for why Elizabeth had no children?

Infertile and old, two circumstances that weren't likely going to change. It seems that for Elizabeth, family was a source of both joy and pain. God had blessed her with a faithful family, yet with no children. It's one of those strange paradoxes of life when a woman who places great importance on family can't have one of her own. Elizabeth was blessed beyond belief—and also burdened. Does this sound familiar? What blessings has God given you? Has He given you a supportive family? a husband who's a strong believer? a career that challenges you? children who delight you?

You may also have pain in your life right now. Maybe your extended family has caused you pain. Or your husband has. Or your children. Or maybe, like Elizabeth, you're struggling with infertility. List your unique blessings and unique burdens. Are any of these both a blessing and a burden to you?

None of these problems is too big for God. You are His daughter, and He wants to comfort you in your pain. He wants to rejoice with you in your blessings. He wants to be right in the middle of your life, paradoxes and all. Meet Him at the center of your life, and trust that He will guide you with His Word and His love.

Pray

Heavenly Father, You have blessed me in many ways, ways that I take for granted. Thank You for giving me my life, my home, and for nourishing me. Thank You for the very personal ways that You've blessed me, God. You are good. Give me Your comfort, Lord. Help me experience Your peace. In Your Son's name I pray. Amen.

Miraculous Fertility

If there's one area of women's lives that causes us the extremes of pain and joy, it's our fertility. We fall into three categories when it comes to planning our families: waiting, trying, or done. It's amazing that every woman in her childbearing years knows exactly which one she fits into at any given time—although sometimes her husband isn't sure. But you know what's even more amazing? Even when we think we know exactly where we fit in the child-bearing spectrum, God always has surprises for us.

Elizabeth probably would have placed herself squarely in the "done" category, even though she hadn't started her family. Because she was advanced in years, she would have given up on having a baby. She was too old. Yet this was the perfect time for her soon-to-be son to introduce the world to its long-awaited Savior. It was the precise moment that God placed her in Mary's life as an inspiration.

If you're struggling with infertility, think of Elizabeth and the specific and deliberate timing that God had for her family. Conception is a miracle, and God performs miracles at the exact right time, *His* time. Like Elizabeth, you may have placed yourself in one category, but God has reason to put you into another. Trust His perfect timing and put your faith in Him through prayer.

Let's take a closer look at the miracle God performed for Elizabeth and her husband, Zechariah, just when they had given up hope.

Right Place, Right Time

In Luke 1:8–10, we meet Zechariah on one of the most important days of his life. He was serving in the temple as the priest before God, an honor that was probably the highlight of his personal and professional life. He was chosen by lot for this rare privilege. Only fifty-six priests officiated in the temple each day, and twenty-eight more were needed on the Sabbath. To burn the incense, Zechariah would have been chosen from about twenty thousand priests. After this important day, he would be retired from the lot forever. This was his day, the pinnacle of his career as a priest, to enter the Holy Place and burn incense to God.

As we learn in verse 10, a huge group of people waited outside for Zechariah to finish. Can you picture the drama of this scene? It wasn't like churches today, where dozens (or hundreds) of us gather in the sanctuary and receive the body and blood of our Savior. In Zechariah's day, the priest was the representative for the people. He alone could enter the inner part of the temple while the throng of worshipers waited for him to offer the sacrifice and return with the blessing for them.

3. a. Read verses 11–25. As Zechariah burns the incense, he makes a special prayer request. We know what was on his heart by what he prays for at this important moment in his life. What does he ask God for?

   b. When Gabriel appears to Zechariah, the angel announces his prayer request for a child would be granted. By what happens next, we can guess that Zechariah didn't fully believe God would give them a baby. What does Zechariah ask the angel in verse 18?

c. What is Gabriel's response?

Wow, what a scene! Here, in this quiet, reverential moment filled with holiness and God's presence, an angel suddenly appeared and completely filled the Holy Place in the temple! If this didn't take old Zechariah's breath away, Gabriel's news did. What was this glorious angel promising? He would be a father? Elizabeth would have a baby? Impossible! She was too old!

It was easier for Zechariah to believe that God *could* do the impossible than that God *would* do the impossible. Does that seem strange to you? Maybe not. Zechariah's response describes my faith perfectly: lots of hope, not nearly enough faith. Although I believe that nothing is impossible with God—there's plenty of evidence of it in Scripture—I live in a broken world that is filled with disappointment. This world is where people I love let me down and where I let myself down, where sin taints everything and where there are lots of impossible situations we cannot find solutions to. I *want* to believe God will work through these impossible situations, but I can't. In my little mind, God surely isn't big enough to conquer problems like infertility and old age. How would He?

This is exactly Zechariah's doubt. Although he was righteous and blameless, although he had enough hope to imagine that God could do something, he didn't have enough faith to see how. The good news, of course, is that

God can and He did. About nine months later, Elizabeth gave birth to John.

The good news for you, sister, is that God can and will and has done the impossible. He did it when He sent His Son to die for you to forgive your sins and reconcile you to your heavenly Father. And this same Father still does the impossible today. Pray that God will accomplish His will. Go ahead, ask the impossible of God. He loves you. He will work through your life to deliver the exact right circumstances for you, His daughter.

The Mentor and the Mentee

What a crazy and wonderful time the next nine months must have been for Elizabeth. She was finally pregnant, but she kept it private for the first five months, knowing the news would shock her community. Imagine the strange scene in their house the first two trimesters of her pregnancy. Zechariah couldn't say anything, and Elizabeth wasn't saying anything about her miracle pregnancy to her family and friends. Did she quietly treasure all this? Was she bursting with the news?

In the next scene in Elizabeth's story, a visit from her much younger cousin Mary, we see that she was very ready to share her good news.

4. a. Read verses 26–38. What second announcement does Gabriel make, this time to Mary?

b. Read verse 26 again. How does Luke mark the timing of Gabriel's announcement?

c. Read verses 36 and 37. What proof does Gabriel use to show Mary that nothing is impossible with God?

The news of Elizabeth's pregnancy must have provided peace of mind to Mary. If she was at all worried about how she was pregnant, Elizabeth's would have been proof that both were indeed from God.

Read verses 39–45, one of my favorite stories in the Bible. Here we see the sisterhood of these two relatives, these believers, as they celebrate God's good news together.

5. What do we learn about their relationship in verses 39 and 40?

6. Read verses 41–45 again.

What miracle of the Holy Spirit happens next?

Can't you just hear the women's joy and friendship through the text? Elizabeth is jubilant to see Mary—and see the miracle that God had performed. A Savior! *The* Savior! He was coming! Mary would give birth to Him!

7. Read verses 46–56. Mary was excited too.

How does Mary respond to Elizabeth's prediction she would give birth to the Savior of the world?

God gives us women the strong instinct to read feelings. Look closely at the way Mary and Elizabeth behave in each other's company: like giddy friends, exclaiming their news in breathless excitement. Christian friendships are a special gift from God. With other believing women, we can ask questions about the Bible, pray together, encourage one another with Scripture, and tell one another about the ways Christ works in our lives.

Share with your group or write here about special friendships God has given you. How have these sister Christians helped you grow in your faith?

A Baby Named John

In the brief glimpse we have of Elizabeth's pregnancy, we see that she certainly seems to be enjoying it. We can imagine that as the nine months drew to a close, her excitement would have been coupled with wonder. As a devout student of the Scriptures, Elizabeth would have known of other women with miraculous pregnancies, like Sarah with Isaac and Hannah with Samuel. And of course, her sweet little cousin Mary was miraculously pregnant with the Christ Child. She must have wondered what special plans God had for her own miracle baby.

8. Reread verses 14–17. What did the angel tell Zechariah about whom John would be?

9. Read verses 57–80. How did Elizabeth's family and friends welcome John?

10. What did Zechariah and Elizabeth do when John was eight days old? What does this tell you about them?

11. Why did Elizabeth and Zechariah name their son John, which means "the Lord has shown favor"?

John's conception and birth had been full of mystery. There was Zechariah's odd behavior when he was serving at the temple and his subsequent speechlessness. Then a pregnancy for old Elizabeth. Now faithful Zechariah and Elizabeth were giving their child a strange name, one that wasn't from their family.

If God's intent was to draw attention to John—and it was!—His plan was working perfectly. Now, with another group present, Zechariah started singing a song of praise that could only be inspired by the Holy Spirit. What did it all mean?

12. Look closely at Zechariah's prophecy in Luke 1:67–79. What is his message about what God is doing?

Through the very moment of John's conception, through Elizabeth's miraculous pregnancy and her connection with Mary, through John recognizing Jesus as the Son of God, through Zechariah's prophecy, John's life pointed to Jesus Christ.

As the mother of such a special son, Elizabeth must have wondered what her calling was. How would she parent such an important boy? By looking at her story through the lens of relationships, we can see exactly what her calling was. Elizabeth, older and wiser than Mary, would be a mentor to her younger cousin. As a mother chosen by God to birth and raise a special son, she would be an inspiration to the impressionable young girl.

Messenger and Messiah

We don't know if Elizabeth lived long enough to see her John tell crowds about Jesus or to see him baptize the Messiah. She probably didn't live to see Jesus, her cousin Mary's little baby, die on the cross. But we do know that the ministry of Elizabeth's miracle child changed the world.

13. Read Isaiah 40:3. What was John the Baptist's calling?

In this culture, a messenger would come before a king to make sure everything was ready for him. The messenger ordered the people to level the roads, clear away thorns, and then he announced the king's arrival.

14. Read Matthew 3. How did John prepare the people for the coming Messiah?

Although Elizabeth was probably gone, we know that Mary lived to see these grown cousins work together to tell the world about the fulfillment of God's prophecy of the Messiah and the hope the Messiah brought. What a uniquely special opportunity God gave the mothers of Jesus and John to share their pregnancies together. And this was the perfect time and place for Elizabeth to be the mentoring mom.

God Loves the Mentoring Mom

For thousands of years, one generation of Christian women has shared work, laughter, support, lessons, and love with the next generation. God has blessed us with strong relationships to support each other.

15. In his letter to Titus, Paul explained how older women in the Church should mentor younger women. Read Titus 2:3–5. How should older women serve as mentors?

16. Read 1 Corinthians 11:1.
    What simple mentoring principle did Paul teach?

Sister in Christ, you are blessed to be a blessing. Consider this your invitation to share your blessings with another woman through a mentoring relationship. As you follow Christ's example and Paul's direction, build relationships with other women, invite them to worship, serve side by side with them. Teach them.

17. God has given you special talents and joys that you can share with the next generation of women. Read 1 Corinthians 12. What are your spiritual gifts? How can you share them to bless those younger or newer in the faith?

18. Read Ephesians 4:14–16. How can you bless others— maybe your own children—with the lessons you've learned?

Are you an example to another woman? Is an older woman mentoring you? How do you see God working through these relationships to teach you? How do you train younger women to love their husbands and children? Discuss your thoughts with your group or jot them here.

Pray

Father, I want to follow the example of Christ, but I need Your Holy Spirit to strengthen my faith and witness. Help me to share Your love with others through the enrichment of Your Spirit and the example of Your Son. In His name I pray. Amen.

MARY
The Accepting Mom

Very Important Woman?

Have you met this woman?

She likes to feel important. Have coffee with her and she'll tell you what's wrong with the world, the president, television, magazines, and even the book you're reading. Next, she'll fill you in about what's wrong with your friends, whose husband isn't loving enough and whose is too much so, which one is harsh and which is a pushover. She'll let you know in no uncertain terms which friend doesn't deserve the nice things she has, which one doesn't have a good life or any common sense or any clue or any fun. After that, she's on to others in the coffee shop—who looks cheap or frumpy, who is too fat or too skinny, the damage they're doing to themselves by eating this but not that.

By the time she's on to her own husband and what's wrong with her kids, you're exhausted trying to keep up with her critique. But she's still going strong. Now she wants to hear about you and your family. She's on your side. And if anyone has been unfair to you, she's quick to point out what's wrong with them.

That does feel better, doesn't it? Just one cappuccino with this woman and you're also important. You had been feeling down. Not anymore. Now you feel like a very important person—until you leave and realize the importance was fake. Suddenly, you deflate. Come to think of it, you didn't feel that great when you were with her. Despite this, you accept her next coffee invitation because it is nice to feel important, even if it's just for a short while.

You deserve that, don't you?

Here's a thought: maybe you don't just know this woman, maybe you *are* this woman. Maybe you're so addicted to critiquing everyone else that you don't realize how downgrading it is to them. And you certainly don't see the damage it's doing to yourself or your relationships.

Especially your relationship with God.

Do you know, dear sister, that you are very important already? To God, you're precious. He created you, He knows you, He redeemed you through the agony and death of His Son. God can see right through you, directly to your soul. He knows your worries. He knows why you don't feel accepted, why you don't feel appreciated.

And God doesn't want you to see yourself that way.

Oh, no. God wants you to see yourself just like He

sees you—through the lens of the Savior who loves you. He doesn't see you as needy, wasting time and energy by bloating yourself up with fake importance. (That's Satan talking.) God wants you to recognize the gifts He's given you so you can humble yourself and serve those people who are hurting. You can show them who Christ is by loving them.

This is a good time to meet Mary. She was a very important person. The angel Gabriel called her "favored" (Luke 1:28). Mary's relative Elizabeth announced she was "blessed . . . among women" (v. 42). Mary herself praises God that generations will "call [her] blessed" (v. 48).

And yet she was humble.

Who, ME?

God chose Mary for the highest honor any woman— any person—ever had and ever would experience.

She wasn't a random choice. God isn't haphazard, and He doesn't make mistakes. Thousands of generations before Mary was born, God already knew the specific girl and the precise time and the perfect place and the exact circumstances through which He would deliver the Savior of the world.

Who would have guessed it would be through Mary? Each faithful woman we've studied must have hoped that she would be the one. When Eve found out she was pregnant, she wondered if she would give birth to the Redeemer that God had promised her (Genesis 4:1). Did Sarah also hope to be the one? God had promised Abraham generations of descendants (12:2). Would their baby Isaac be the Savior? Think about how Rebekah asked God about her pregnancy (25:22–26). Did she hope His answer would be that she would give birth to the most special Child? Jochebed knew that her son, Moses, was special (Exodus 2:2). Did she think he would save all people, even the Egyptians? Hannah was blessed with a child she set apart for God (1 Samuel 1:11). Did she believe he would save the world from its sin? God gave Bathsheba's son Solomon the name Jedidiah, "beloved of the LORD" (2 Samuel 12:25). Did she wonder if he would redeem Israel to its God? Elizabeth's pregnancy had started so strangely. Was God delivering the Christ through her old womb?

Any of these women might have accepted God's calling to be the mother of the Lord, but He chose Mary.

1. Reading Luke 3:23–38, we think Mary may have come from the right family herself (and her fiancé certainly did). The house of Judah may have led right to her, the mother of God. Now read Isaiah 7:14–17. What did the prophecy proclaim about who would give birth to the Savior? Where would Immanuel be born?

So, after many centuries, God was ready to complete the work He had promised Eve, the first mother, and all generations after her. The long-promised Savior was coming, but from the least expected woman. She may be the youngest, poorest, and least prepared for motherhood of the women we've studied.

And probably the one who didn't ask, "Who, ME?"

Not Me, You

Perhaps we see Mary's humble spirit best at the annunciation, the moment that Gabriel announced she would give birth to the Christ child.

2. Read Luke 1:29. What was Mary's reaction to Gabriel's strange greeting?

In verses 30–33, Gabriel tells her the astounding news that God had chosen her to give birth to the Messiah. We don't see Mary pat herself on the back, relish her lineage, or glory in how well she'd kept God's Law. Mary doesn't make this thing about her; it's about God. She doesn't doubt what God can do, she simply wants to know *how* He'll do it. A good question, since she's never had sex.

3. After Gabriel explains the miracle God will perform, look at Mary's reaction in verse 38. What does she say?

Mary still hasn't used this information to make herself important. She was humble before Gabriel arrived with the biggest news in the history of the world, and she remains humble. She simply accepts God's miracle as fact and identifies herself as a lowly servant in His plan.

I can't help but see a lesson here for all of us. Mary

made herself small, flat, empty, and God filled her. The Holy Spirit filled her right up with His Son, the Savior of the world. What about you? What would He fill you with if there was less of your *self* taking up space? if you thought of yourself only as His servant?

4. Read Matthew 23:12. What does Jesus tell us happens when we puff ourselves up with pride?

You don't need to make yourself important. God already has done this in the most significant way possible.

5. Read 1 Peter 2:9. How do you know you're a very important person to God?

Every day, over and over, He chooses *you*. You don't have to wonder who you are or try to be someone you aren't meant to be. Because of your Baptism, you know you are God's child, the most important person you can be. Delight in your identity, daughter of the King. Bask in your position with the confidence that His kingdom is yours and He chose you to be there. Our struggles (and yes, despite all of this, each of us still has plenty) cannot change our special positions as chosen, loved, wanted children of God.

What She Asked, What She Didn't Ask

Based on the short conversations the angel Gabriel had with Zechariah and Mary, readers would forever think of these believers differently. Both simply asked a question, but God punished Zechariah (Luke 1:20) for his, and Mary is remembered for her faith.

The message that a baby was on the way was radically different news for Zechariah than it was for Mary. Zechariah was a respected priest who had been married for decades. The community had been expecting him and Elizabeth to have a baby for years. Their family and friends *wanted* to see Zechariah with a son. Elizabeth and Zechariah were wise, blameless, and devout in following the Lord. They only lacked children to fill with their love and faith—the couple was beyond ready.

But young Mary, maybe only thirteen, was not married (almost, but not yet). She was a risk. If you've mothered teenagers, you know what I mean. Until there was a wedding, no one wanted to see Mary with a baby bump.

But it was more serious than that.

If there was any hint at all that Mary had been doing postmarital activities premaritally, the community would shun her. Especially if Joseph made the point that those activities hadn't been with him. If Joseph was angry enough about the situation, he could report her crime and have her stoned.

A baby would bless Zechariah, the old, married priest. A baby would burden Mary, the young, unmarried virgin.

6. a. Read verse 18. What does Zechariah ask when Gabriel tells him that Elizabeth will have a baby?

b. Read verse 34. What does Mary ask?

c. How was her question different from Zechariah's?

Mary's reaction to a miracle—an inconvenient miracle, even—shows her as the accepting mom. Think of the questions she *doesn't* ask: Won't Joseph leave me? Won't I be killed? Who will take care of me? What will my parents say? Can I handle this? Won't my Son have to die to be the world's Savior? Why do *I* have to be this special mother? Why me?

These are questions I know I would have asked, doubts that this sinful sister would have had.

Right in the middle of what could have been some really bad news, Mary called herself a "servant of the Lord" (v. 38). But to be His servant, she would have to trust God and submit to Him. Read Psalm 18:2. God is your rock and your fortress. He is your stronghold. Think about these words that Mary may have memorized as a student of the Scriptures.

7. a. What do you think these words meant to Mary?

b. What do the words of Psalm 18 mean to you?

Pray

Lord, thank You for Your protection. Thank You for being my stronghold I can trust completely. Help me to look to You every single day. Help me to believe Your promises. In Your Son's name I pray. Amen.

God, the Same Yesterday and Today

Our three-year-old son's questions about God show a lot about how much (or how little) he understands about his Creator: What does God do when He's bored? What toys does God play with? What time does God go to bed?

To my little boy, God is just a big boy. The Almighty is different from him only because He lives in heaven and can do miracles. To my son's young, developing faith, God has all the same problems that he does.

We all do this to God, don't we? We make our Father human; we imagine He has our same struggles; we assign our hang-ups to Him. God gets tired of hearing the same things from us over and over, doesn't He? God runs out of patience with us, right? God is comfortable providing a mediocre faith for us, true?

Not so! God is more merciful than even the most disgusting sinner could hope for. God is more powerful than even the most lost soul could want. God is more patient and more faithful than our distracted human brains can imagine.

And God doesn't change. He doesn't go through seasons of His life. He doesn't mature. He was the same yesterday as He is today (Hebrews 13:8). He was the same when Mary, with the Christ Child in her belly, sang her praise song about Him in Elizabeth's living room two thousand years ago. He is the same right now, in your life.

8. a. Read Luke 1:49. What does Mary praise about God in this verse?

b. What does she praise in verse 50?

c. in verses 51–52?

d. in verse 53?

e. in verses 54–55?

Share with your group or write here how Mary's humble song of praise inspires you. What inconceivable qualities are you glad that God has yesterday, today, and forever?

Joy and Pain

Mary was a devout believer. When Jesus was forty days old, this bleary-eyed new mommy took her baby to the temple. According to Jewish Law, she needed purification from giving birth. Jesus was the firstborn boy to Mary and Joseph, which meant He was set aside for the Lord. Mary and Joseph had to offer a pair of turtledoves as a sacrifice.

At the temple was an old man named Simeon. The Holy Spirit had revealed to him that he would see the Christ before he died. Enter Mary holding tiny baby Jesus! Old Simeon's words must have surprised Mary.

9. a. Read Luke 2:29–35. What part of Simeon's prophecy would have brought Mary joy?

b. And what did Simeon prophesy that would have been painful for her?

What do you think Mary thought about Simeon's words? Did she take them literally, that she would also be stabbed in the heart? Did she remember the prophecy in Isaiah 53:3—the Savior would be "despised and rejected . . . acquainted with grief"? Did she remember Isaiah 53:10—it would be "the will of the LORD to crush [the Savior]"?

Did Mary freeze on those temple steps, rigid with the weight of realization? Her Son, the precious child she held in her arms, would suffer terribly so that He could bring hope to the suffering. Her six-week-old infant would endure a difficult life and gruesome death.

Could Mary accept all that?

Perhaps she didn't think about all of this in that moment. Mary was taking her first shaky steps of motherhood. Like any first-time mom, she was trying to understand the delicate balance of marching with confidence and tiptoeing with fear. Isn't it by the grace of God that we mothers understand our roles in one-day-at-time chunks, with only a bit of light to shine on our next steps? From the Scriptures, Mary knew more about her son's future than other moms know about their own children's lives to come, but we see this same grace of God throughout her story. From radical joy to intense sadness, Mary was the accepting mom. She trusted God, even when she could have been terrified.

The night Jesus was born, although both miraculous and blessed, must have also been a bit scary for Mary. She surely looked forward to the support when her time came. The women of her family and midwives of the community would coach her, literally holding her hand. Some traditions hold that her own mother, Anna, would have been present, but the Bible doesn't tell us for sure.

What we do know is that after a long journey, Mary ended up in a stable—no midwives or family in sight. What a night that must have been, one so miraculous Mary couldn't grasp all that had happened. No wonder she "pondered [these things] in her heart" (Luke 2:19). She must have been scrambling to understand them.

When Jesus was twelve years old and His family traveled to the temple, Mary was surprised to find Him teaching the teachers. When Jesus told her He was "in [His] Father's house" (Luke 2:49), she was confused, but the Bible tells us that she "treasured up all these things in her heart" (v. 51). For the fourth time in Scripture, someone told Mary who her Son really was. Can't you imagine her watching Jesus as He grew up and contemplating, wondering, hoping, praying for her firstborn?

At the Cana wedding, the host family ran out of wine. Mary summoned Jesus, who reprimanded her again, telling her "My hour has not yet come" (John 2:4). Here we see her faith in who her Son was becoming. She told the servants, "Do whatever He tells you" (v. 5).

While we know that Mary was God's faithful, accepting servant throughout her life, there were times that raising this special child would have been painful for her. Read Matthew 12:46–50. Jesus' ministry was growing and attracting the attention of the Jewish law.

Mary went with her other children to talk to Jesus about being careful.

10. What must she have felt when Jesus rebuffed His earthly family?

11. a. Mary was at the foot of the cross and watched her Son die a painful, slow, criminal's death. Read John 19:25–27. What emotions might the accepting mom have felt at this moment?

b. What joy might she have felt?

12. Read Acts 1:14. What evidence do we have that Mary understood Jesus' ministry and sacrifice?

Mary could have earned the title of the accepting mom just for her joyful response to Gabriel's message. But she kept her answer "I am the servant of the Lord" (Luke 1:38) throughout her life. Despite her confusion, she trusted God, contemplating her Son and her role as the mother of the Messiah. She was a humble servant, never a stumbling block to her Son's ministry.

In Isaiah 6:8, God calls Isaiah, and he exclaims, "Here am I! Send me." Did his response inspire Mary when she heard it generations later? Could Isaiah's response also inspire you? Could you also say, "Here am I! Send me"?

Discuss your response with your group, or write it here.

God Loves the Accepting Mom

From the billions of women since Eve, God chose only one to give birth to the Christ Child. Only menopausal Sarah could be Isaac's mother. He chose only faithful Jochebed to be Moses' mom. Old Elizabeth was mother John the Baptist. And Mary would be the mother of God.

Does God still choose women today? Has He chosen you to be the special mother to a child? Or perhaps you are wondering why He would chose you? Doesn't He realize your shortfalls? Doesn't He know about all your issues? about your sin?

Of course He does; He knows you better than anyone else ever will (and that includes you). Yet, God *has* chosen you. To be a mother. To be a friend. To teach children. To help those who desperately need it. To serve others in His name. To be His.

13. Read Ephesians 2:8–10. Why did God create you?

14. Read Romans 8:28. What does God promise us
about doing His work?

God chose you. Yes. *You.* When you were washed in the water of Baptism together with the Word of Christ, God chose you to be His beloved daughter and heir to His kingdom of glory. Even while you were a sinner, God took you into His eternal kingdom.

As Mary watched her Son die on the cross, she accepted that He was the One and she accepted her role in God's plan. May your response to Gabriel's call, dear sister in Christ, be like hers, "Behold, I am the servant of the Lord; let it be to me according to your word" (Luke 1:38).

Pray

Heavenly Father, help me know I am very important to You. Help me live out this wonderful news. Show me the plans You have for me to spread the good news about Your Son. In His name I pray. Amen.

EUNICE AND LOIS
The Nurturing Moms

Real Life Lessons

While writing this study, God gave me the good sense to meet with other moms.

If I hadn't talked to living, breathing moms every week, I'd have stuck my head in a sandpit of research. I thank the Lord for the chance to sit with other moms to commiserate and share the Word. It was the highlight of my week and definitely the best part of this study. Together, we talked and laughed and shared and cried and shared some more. Although we began the *God Loves Moms* study as strangers, we ended as friends.

Through our sharing, there was one biblical truth that grabbed us every week: we reap what we sow. Sometimes this was good news. One mom shared how she'd been praying with her son every night. She's done this since day one—long before he could support his own head, let alone bow it. Now, her elementary-school-age son enthusiastically prays—in public or private—whenever he gets the chance. She'd sown the seeds of prayer, and every time her son turned to God, she reaped them.

Another mom shared a sad story about a value she had inadvertently instilled in her kids. Her daughter loved nice things. Actually, she loved *really* nice things that she couldn't afford. Now, at age twenty-two, the daughter was drowning in serious credit-card debt. Her mom, our dear friend, hadn't meant to teach her child bad spending practices. But over the years, she had faithfully modeled them to her girl.

Many of my Bible study sessions with these moms ended with our marveling that God has entrusted our kids to us. We could teach our children almost anything— to love God or to love the University of Texas football team or to hate church or to pray every night before bed or to eat M&M's every time they got in the car—if we told them to and lived it as an example. Over and over again, we came to the conclusion that only God's Word would make a difference in their lives. Nurturing our kids' faith by taking them to church, reading the Bible to them, teaching them that Jesus loves them, and praying with them are the best habits and messages that influence their lives.

Thank You, Lord, for the stories from this wonderful, fun group of women. Through their colorful testimonies, this mom has seen that we reap what we sow. And nothing is more important than sowing God's Word.

Pioneer Women

When God's Word gets hold of your heart, you want to share it with the world. The Holy Spirit grabbed hold of Paul's heart, and from that moment on, he was off. Paul traveled the world to share the truth with everyone he met. Across hundreds and hundreds of miles, from Jerusalem all the way to Macedonia, Paul told Jews and Greeks that Jesus had come and died and fulfilled the Law completely and perfectly. Jesus Christ was their Savior, who had died for them so they could live!

On one of Paul's trips, he visited Lystra, a remote city. Hittites had settled Lystra thousands of years before, and Hittite descendents still lived there. Over the centuries, several armies, including the Persians, Greeks, and Romans, had invaded and ruled the region.

During Paul's lifetime, Lystra was under Roman rule. The city was strategically located on a high elevation near the foothills of the Tarsus Mountains, so it was an excellent military outpost. Traders also traveled through Lystra and stopped to settle there.

After generations under various powers, Lystra was like a pioneer town, filled with influence from every corner of the world. The culture revolved around pagan gods, and there were very few Jews in the town, not even enough for a place of worship. The closest synagogue was in Iconium, twenty miles away.

The Lycaonians put their faith in the gods of Greek mythology. Archeologists discovered a statue outside of

Lystra of Hermes, dedicated to Zeus. The people had built the statue next to a temple for Zeus.

1. a. Read Acts 14:1–18. What did the confused Lycaonians do when they saw Paul heal a lame man?

   b. How did Paul and Barnabas react to the confused offerings of these people?

   c. Read Acts 14:19–23. What happens next?

An unbelievable story, isn't it? There are some confused people in our world, but have you heard of anything like this? First, the Lycaonians worshiped Paul; then, they helped stone him.

Roman soldiers, Greek scholars, and also Jewish believers—all kinds of people—had gathered in the crowd that day to see the Lycaonians mistreat Paul. Perhaps Eunice and Lois, our nurturing moms, had also gone to the center of the city to hear Paul preach. What did they think about his message that the Messiah had come and had died for their sins? Was Timothy in the crowd to hear Paul and Barnabas? What did he think about their message?

We know the answers by the rest of Timothy's story. By the work of the Holy Spirit, Paul's message of God's grace grabbed hold of Timothy's heart. This young believer listened to Paul, weighed his message against what he knew about the Scriptures, and believed. Not only did Timothy believe, but he also traveled with Paul and ministered alongside him.

From this confused, pagan culture, a city without enough believers for a house of worship, came a pastor for the next generation.

Our world seems just as confused as Lystra, doesn't it? It's hard to hear God's truth over the blaring of false prophets. Sometimes these false prophets are scientists who offer theories as evidence that the Bible isn't true and Christians, therefore, are closed-minded. Sometimes, these prophets are pop culture icons who tell us that believing in God is backward and ridiculous, that we are in control. And sometimes false prophets come in the guise of the religious figures who would have us believe that if we don't have glorious lives in the here and now, we're just not believing hard enough or giving enough or doing enough.

Like Timothy, the next generation is listening. They hear the confused world promising hope and happiness and failing to deliver. This next generation hears us too. They hear us sharing the Gospel truth through the Word of God. They watch us as we worship in church and turn to God in prayer. The next generation sees the hope we have through Jesus Christ.

Like Paul writes to Timothy in his second letter to him, God's Word is for teaching and will equip believers for every good work.

Read 2 Timothy 3:10–17. In your own words, tell what good news you find in Paul's words to Timothy.

When Father Doesn't Know Best

Paul mentions Timothy's grandma Lois and mother, Eunice, only one time. He credits them with teaching young Timothy the Scriptures (2 Timothy 1:5). From this, we know Timothy's mom and grandma believed and shared their faith with Timothy. Was Timothy's family a model of faith in every way?

Nope, dysfunctional. Just like our families today. Yes, Grandma Lois was a firm believer, whose husband may have died. But Eunice? She married a Greek, a nonbeliever—a circumstance that would affect the rest of her life. Perhaps no other decision could jeopardize the faith of her children more than to marry someone who rejected God's Word.

2. Read Acts 16:3. How do we know that Timothy's father didn't follow God's commands?

3. Read Genesis 17:9–14. What is the covenant of circumcision?

To Timothy's father, a Greek who might have been raised by pagan worshipers, circumcision was a strange custom done to appease a God he didn't believe in. Lois and Eunice, who knew and believed God's Old Testament promises, must have worried about uncircumcised Timothy. His father hadn't done the duty that God commanded, the duty that connected God's people to Him.

Women didn't have the right to take care of this themselves. Timothy's mom or grandma couldn't have just taken the infant twenty miles to Iconium and insist he be circumcised. Not without his father's permission.

4. Read Acts 16:3–4. What does Paul do when Timothy travels with him to spread the Word of God? Why?

Paul knew how important circumcision was to the Jewish people—after all, it was their covenant with God. He circumcised Timothy as an ancient marketing device to ensure the Jews wouldn't reject the young missionary before they even heard what he had to say.

Maybe Lois and Eunice, Timothy's faithful grandma and mom, were relieved that after all these years, Timothy was finally circumcised. Or maybe they understood Paul's teaching in Galatians 6:15 that Jesus Christ represents our new covenant with God and that circumcision is no longer necessary. Either way, the problem of Timothy's circumcision would have worried these two faithful believers as they taught Timothy about God.

5. Think about marriage today. Why is it important that we as believers marry other believers? Read 2 Corinthians 6:14. What does Paul warn believers against?

When Eunice married a Greek, she joined together forever with a man who didn't see life with the same promises and hope that she did. Think about this in the context of your own life. What choices have you made that could have damaged your faith? How have those choices affected you?

God has given us the responsibility to choose. Of course, as sinners, we often make bad choices, ones that tear us from Him. Through your Baptism, you belong to God. He loves you and claims you as part of His family. You are His, dear sister, even when you make potentially faith-fatal errors. At any time, before, during, or after any decision, you can run to Him, cling to the promises of the cross, and delight in your identity as His daughter.

Sowing the Seeds of God

Isn't it amazing that when Jesus took on human form and came to earth, He didn't just live as the King of kings, displaying His God qualities, to be worshiped and glorified? He could have set Himself up as an exhibit, "Come and see the living and breathing God-man!" As we've seen in the people of Lystra, the culture was well versed in idol worship. Jesus could have lived as the ultimate royalty, convincing people to believe by displaying His power.

But Jesus was different. He didn't demand obedience. Instead, He taught about it. To both His followers and His critics, He explained who God was. To help the people really understand God and His kingdom, Jesus walked hundreds of dirty miles in His sandals to illustrate the kingdom of God.

Actually, Jesus did more than that. He considered how the human mind works, then He used imagery and stories and allegories and very *human* methods to clarify the heavenly Father to the masses.

Perhaps you've heard the parable of the sower. In Matthew, Mark, and Luke, Jesus uses the imagery of seeds and plants and fruit to help His agriculturally-minded audience understand why some believe God's Word and others don't. Jesus' parable of the sower helps us understand today too. What makes believers? Why will some embrace the God's Word while others will reject it? Is this our fault as teachers?

6. a. Read Matthew 13:3–8, 18–23.

   In the parable, what is the seed?

   b. What do the seeds that fall on the road represent?

   c. What do the seeds that fall on the rocks represent?

   d. What do the seeds that fall on thorns represent?

   e. What do the seeds that fall on good soil represent?

No one felt the rejection of God's Word more acutely that Jesus. Here He was, God Himself, explaining to His creation who they were and how much their Father loved them. And yet some cynics looked right at Jesus, shook their heads, and walked away. Some hated Him for claiming He was Christ. Eventually, these scoffers killed Him.

Jesus didn't take it personally. But because He knew rejection would hurt His disciples, He made sure they understood that belief was out of their hands. As humans, we can't make anyone believe. Satan will interfere. Cynicism will rule the sinful human mind. Sin will convince us that money and science are better investments for our hearts than an invisible God.

You probably don't have to look beyond your own family to understand Jesus' parable. Why is it that some children hear the Word of God and embrace it? They live their faith; they defend God to critics. They lead their lives as a testimony to His Word.

And then there are their siblings. How can it be that this other child, who also was baptized, heard the Word of God, said nightly prayers, and went to church every Sunday, would refuse to believe?

Is this happening to you, dear sister? Have you shared the Word of God with family and friends only to have them reject it? Have you invested your time and your instruction in someone who just couldn't believe? Share your experiences with the group or write about them here.

7. Read 2 Timothy 1:5–7. Paul credits Eunice
   and Lois by name for nurturing Timothy.
   What bad soil were these two women dealing with?

Despite this rocky soil, these two women persevered. These nurturing moms continued to teach the truth about God, even when they weren't sure if their words would have any effect on Timothy.

Two thousand years later, we know the rest of the story. The seeds of faith settled in Timothy's heart and bore fruit. Eunice and Lois's work wasn't in vain. Timothy grew up to be a believer and a powerful evangelist of God's Word.

Pray

Dear Lord, You understand the frustrations of the evangelist. You've seen sin choke Your Word. Father, help me share Your Gospel promises with the next generation, those who need the assurance of Your grace. Strengthen me with Your Holy Spirit. In Your Son's name I pray. Amen.

Timothy, the Nurtured Child

Timothy grew up to be an evangelist, a pastor, and a leader in the Early Christian Church. Paul wrote two personal letters to Timothy.

8. Read 2 Timothy 1:2. What does Paul call Timothy?

At this time in the history of the Church, pagan families would often reject relatives who became Christians. When this happened, believers adopted one another into new spiritual families. Paul naming Timothy as his son was common nomenclature. Timothy's own father, a man who didn't believe in God or Jesus, might have rejected his son, the outspoken evangelist. When Paul named himself as Timothy's spiritual father, he took on the duty of caring for Timothy and continued Eunice and Lois's work of nurturing the young man's faith.

In Paul and Timothy's relationship, we see something like our modern concept of godparents. At Baptism, godparents promise to nurture the infant's faith. Although the child's parents might be believers, godparents accept responsibility also to teach the baby about our Father's kingdom and to pray for that child by name.

We see an extraordinary example of a godfather and godson in Paul and Timothy's relationship. Timothy traveled with Paul on several missionary journeys, giving his mentor plenty of opportunity to teach him. Throughout

Paul's ministry, he helped guide Timothy to be a strong leader of the Early Christian Church.

9. a. Read 2 Timothy 4:7–8. Before his death, Paul wrote some of his last words to Timothy. What were they?

    b. Paul and Timothy had served together for years. How would Paul's final words have been a powerful encouragement to the younger pastor?

Teach the Little Children

10. Read Deuteronomy 11:18. What is God's command about how we should teach His Word?

11. Read Proverbs 22:6. What simple truth does God tell us about teaching our kids to love God?

12. Read Mark 10:13–16; Matthew 18:2–6. Jesus reminded the disciples of an obvious truth. Children, more innocent and accepting than adults, believe more easily. How is this an encouragement to those of us teaching the next generation about their Savior?

13. a. Read Hebrews 12:9–11.

How do we teach our children spiritual discipline?

b. What is the "peaceful fruit of righteousness" that's promised in verse 11?

Share with your group, or write here, other ideas for how you can teach God's Word to the next generation.

God Loves the Nurturing Moms

14. Read Luke 12:32–34.

What point does Jesus make in verse 34?

Jesus taught it; Paul preached it; Timothy lived it. You reap what you sow. Actually, this isn't only a biblical principal. Behavioral experts, educational psychologists, and parenting coaches all agree that your children will learn what you model, what you invest in, what you treasure. All mothers learn that children are mimics and sponges. When He chooses us to be mothers, God gives us the exciting opportunity to share His Word with the next generation. It's His command; it's His request; it's His invitation.

It's our privilege.

Telling the next generation the truth that their heavenly Father created them and loves them gives them hope and understanding. As adults, we know the pain that exists in the sin-filled world. It can be overwhelming. Look at a newborn child, and you may think about the exhilarating events life has to offer.

You may also think about the hurt and pain and sin the child will endure. A bully will tease him. This child will endure a potentially serious sickness. Someone will hate him. Satan will try to tear this child from his Father. He will love someone that doesn't love him back. At the darkest moment of this child's life, he will be faced with the most threatening question: what do I believe?

The answer to that question, an answer you can share with him today, may be the words that make all the difference in his life.

God equips you to share hope with the children in your life. He has not just equipped you, but He has also empowered you. No, He hasn't only equipped and empowered you to share His love with the next generation, but He's also commanded you. But know this too: because this calling is from God, He will bless your efforts to share the good news of the saving Gospel. And then He takes it from there. Your words will not return empty. You might not see it, but you can be sure because God promises it.

Look at the example we have through Eunice and Lois. Although they faced challenges—an unbelieving father and a radical, pagan community—this faithful mother and grandmother believed that God's Word would make the difference for Timothy. By sharing His love with him, they gave him a hope and a future. And by the work of the Holy Spirit, this young, fertile soil bore the fruit of their teaching by sharing God's Word with generations and generations of believers.

Pray

Heavenly Father, You know the struggles I face in this world. I'm not always a good example of Your love. I don't always model my faith. Forgive me; let me be certain of Your forgiveness. Empower me to share Your Word with the world, including my own family. In Your Son's name I pray. Amen.

WIDOW OF NAIN
The Grieving Mom

Room 3425

My friend Lindy Mertins experienced unexpected grief when her daughter Finley was born. She found herself mourning the child that Finley isn't and embracing the child that Finley is. Here's Lindy's story, in her own words.

inley Renee joined our lives two and a half weeks early on December 9, 2008. The moment she was placed on my chest, I lovingly examined all six pounds, fourteen ounces of her through tear-filled eyes. At age 35, I was finally a mom.

I don't recall the exact moment my heart began to feel an unexpected ache. But in the quiet of Room 3425, my new-mom instinct overwhelmed me and I recognized that something about my precious baby girl was different. The baby I'd carried for nearly nine months had eyes that were similar in shape to those of an actor who played Corky on the early-1990s television series *Life Goes On*. And the ache in my heart grew as I nervously wondered if anyone else had noticed. Hours passed when I finally asked the question.

"Does it look like Finley has Down syndrome?"

The pediatrician confirmed my heart's fear less than twenty-four hours later.

Had I known in the quiet of Room 3425 what I know now, the unexpected diagnosis of Down syndrome would not have made my heart ache. Finley is a gift. Down syndrome is a gift. And God knew it even as He formed her in my womb and safely delivered her to me. I no longer grieve the baby I thought I was going to have. Rather, I embrace and celebrate the baby I was meant to have in sweet Finley. She has helped me to be a more patient, understanding, flexible, and compassionate woman. And God used her diagnosis to bring me back around to seeking Him in all that I do in my life.

Less than a year after Finley's birth, God would once again challenge my reliance upon Him when my husband's infidelity brought an end to our marriage. Sadly, Finley will never remember a time when she lived with her mom and dad together as a family. Yet I believe that Down syndrome will forever protect her from fully understanding the depth of this type of betrayal and the pain of divorce. God knew how to set the stage for what was to come.

Finley is now a healthy and happy two-year-old who just happens to have an extra chromosome. And for that, I'm eternally thankful. For without it, she wouldn't be my Finley Renee.

Lindy's story captures the unexpected grief so many of us moms face. We dream about our children's future—who they'll become, the relationship we'll have with them—only to be devastated when reality proves differently. A teen daughter who announces she's pregnant. A son with an addiction. A stillborn baby. Several miscarriages. A daughter with an extra chromosome. A son killed by the split-second turn of an oncoming car.

Why? we ask God. *This isn't what I expected. This isn't what I deserve. This isn't what I can handle.*

These are the questions a widow might have asked two thousand years ago when her son died, leaving her alone and hopeless. We don't know if this widow in Nain ever found out why, because instead of seeing answers, she saw that our God is a loving, powerful God who has overcome every trial imaginable, including death.

At one of the most painful moments of her life, this widow understood what most moms spend a lifetime struggling to comprehend: God is always compassionate. He is always powerful. He is always good.

Even when we don't understand how or why.

A Hole

In AD 30, women could face circumstances so dire that we can't begin to comprehend them. Yes, of course we experience tragedy today. Suffering through a divorce or death of a spouse is heartbreaking. But today, widows and divorcées have options: child support, welfare, support groups, insurance benefits.

Not the case two thousand years ago. If a woman's husband died, her life could quickly spiral into hopelessness. There was no honorable employment for women. There were no food stamps. No WIC programs. Family and friends might help the widow, but she was at their mercy and whim and economics. And life would be so lonely for her. The culture centered around family; without a spouse, she would be without companionship. Her situation would be dire. Because a widow's life was so bleak, it was vital for God's community to help her. In Mosaic Law, God established the practice of the kinsman-redeemer. Remember Ruth? Boaz was her kinsman-redeemer. By marrying her, he kept her from a life of poverty and loneliness.

1. Read James 1:27. How does James define religion?

Caring for widows was such an important act of charity, James equates it with religion itself.

2. a. Read Luke 7:11–17, the story of the widow of Nain. Not only was this woman a widow, but her situation was even more tragic. Why?

b. Read verse 12 again. What details does Luke reveal that show her desperation?

Alone. Grieving. Vulnerable.

This woman had endured the death of her husband, and now she lost her son too. What more could happen to her? Where was God? If God loved her, how could He have allowed this to happen? How could He have *made* this happen? How could her son, once full of life and breath, now be stretched out, silent and still in death? She must have asked, "Why me, God? After everything else, now this? Why me?" Have you ever felt this hopeless? Has your own life spiraled into a pit that caused you to ask, "Why me?"

I hate to imagine the desperation any of you might be facing right now. Are you suffering through a financial tragedy? a divorce? Are you battling an addiction? Have you slipped into the darkness of depression?

Or maybe one of your children is causing you pain. Has their situation become so tragic that you can only ask, "Why, God? Why?"

If you have a hole of hopelessness, a chasm in your soul, I can only say that I've been there too. I've felt your sadness. I've tried everything I could think of to fill the vacuous space and feel peace again. I've tried to stuff the hole full of things, full of meaningless relationships, full of pride. I've tried to deny that there was any hole in my life. I've filled my hole with bitterness. I've turned away from God.

It's taken years for me to understand what the widow learned that day in Nain. The God who loves you is compassionate toward you. Through faith in Him, through the Holy Spirit, through the mercy of Jesus Christ, He offers you peace and healing that will fill that hole caused by tragedy, disappointment, and grief.

Your Lord, who created you and loves you, sees the holes in your life and He grieves at your pain. He wants you to turn toward Him. He doesn't want you to cover yourself in bitterness. He doesn't want sin to blind you from hope in Him. Ever. His peace, so powerful it surpasses our human understanding, permeates your deepest and darkest holes.

Pray

Heavenly Father, I've known terrible pain. I don't understand how or why I ended up in this place. But I know You love me and You are here with me. You are compassionate and powerful, Lord. Help me see Your grace. Help me trust You. Forgive me and give me peace for Jesus' sake. Amen.

Jesus, the Compassionate Man

In the widow's story, we meet Jesus as a man, teacher, and healer. In this story, we also see two of His divine characteristics: He is compassionate and He is powerful.

These two characteristics of our Lord are evident in every other story of every other biblical mother we've met. God is powerful; He has overcome every sin, including death. God is compassionate; He wants us to experience His total peace.

3. Read Luke 4:38–41; 6:6–11; 7:1–10.
   What miracle did Jesus perform over and over?

Jesus traveled from community to community, healing the lame, the blind, the sick, the desperate. Crowds saw His power as He transformed the sick to be well. They also saw His compassion.

4. Read Luke 7:13 again. What does Jesus feel?
   What does He say?

The word Luke uses is the Greek word *splangchni-zomai* (try saying that three times fast). It means moved from the bowels. Jesus felt His innards (or what we would call His heart today) yearn. Amazing! The man is more powerful than sin and death and the devil, and His heart is wrenched for a hurting mother.

Read Matthew 9:35–38. What strikes you about Jesus' compassion? Discuss your impressions with your group, or write them here.

Jesus visited multitudes of people. He saw how lost they were; He felt compassion for them and healed them. Think about that. Jesus, God of all, saw the people's needs and filled them.

5. a. Read Matthew 9:37. What does Jesus tell His disciples?

b. In your own words, what is that harvest?
Who are the laborers?

Jesus sees us, His sheep, when we're lost and hurting. He seeks us, and He provides what we need. Love. Peace. Hope. Forgiveness. Redemption. That's the message we can share with the world. You don't have to live in pain; your Father loves you and offers you peace and hope.

Where Is God Now?

If you want to share this hope with someone, tell them the widow's story. Reduced to its most basic elements, the story is about a hurting person and her compassionate God.

Imagine that day at the town gate of Nain.

First, the hurting woman. The widow slowly made her way through the town. She was crying, desperate. Surrounding her was a crowd. Women from the community would have led the mob, wailing loudly. Neighborhood men would have taken turns carrying the bier with the body of her dead son. The loud, sobbing crowd was headed outside of town to the cave tomb where the woman's dead husband was probably also buried.

And her loving God. That day in Nain, there was another crowd. Jesus, the charismatic teacher, also led a loud group of people. His ministry had attracted followers. Traveling with Jesus were those who loved Him, like His disciples. There were also those who were curious about Him, who desperately wanted to believe that He was who He said He was. And then there were the skeptics who watched just to see what He would do next.

When these two crowds met at the town gate in Nain, there was a collision between a mother with a hole in her life, a mother who was asking "Why, God?" and . . .

God.

There He was, right in the middle of her pain, meeting her on her way to the hardest moment of her life. God met her and He provided for her. The widow of Nain didn't know why she had to lose her husband and her son, but one person at the edge of the city knew the rest of the story.

Have you had one of these moments? Have you, like Lindy, wondered why your life unfolded in the way you least expected? Has your world ever felt so much like a random, chaotic, cruel place that the idea of a compassionate God seemed impossible?

6. Read Romans 8:28. What does God promise us about the hard times we face?

The world is not random or chaotic. There is no karma or fate or luck. God calls us according to His purpose. He promises all things work for good and His purpose. *All* things. Yes, even in your pain, there will be good. For those of us who love God, He will work through each and every struggle to bring us back to Him.

Like Lindy, who has seen how the blessing of Down syndrome could bring her back to her Father. Like a sister in our Christian community, who tragically lost her daughter last year and now shares her story with teens around the country, asking them if they know their Savior. Like the widow, who was afraid and grieving, only to have her Savior come to meet her and care for her.

We don't have to be afraid or paranoid or insecure. God is stronger than anything we might face. He can and will use our grief to bring us closer to Him. In fact, that's one of the beautiful benefits of the Lord's Supper as we join with the communion of saints.

7. a. Read John 16:33.

What does Jesus promise us about our struggles?

b. Read James 1:2–4.

What opportunity do struggles give us?

c. Read 2 Corinthians 12:9–10.

When we're weak, where can we rest?

God is sovereign. This side of heaven, through sinful, short-sighted human eyes, we can never see the big picture. But we can read the truth right here in Luke's Gospel. God knows our limitations as humans. He wants us to turn to His perfect wisdom and peace. He has wonderful plans for you, plans more outstanding than you could imagine yourself.

Pray

Father, You know me. You know my strengths and weaknesses. You know where I lack faith. Help me to trust You, my Lord, who has provided everything for me. Thank You for caring for me and sending Your Son. In His name I pray. Amen

Second Chances

Those two crowds standing at the town gate of Nain witnessed a powerful miracle. And they didn't keep it to themselves. Luke reports that news about Jesus and what He did for the widow and her son spread throughout Judea and the surrounding country. I can imagine this mother telling the story over and over again to her son, to her neighbors, to anyone who would listen. "I was afraid and hurting, but Jesus was compassionate and mighty. My son was dead, and Jesus gave him life."

By healing her son, Jesus gave this woman a second chance with him. He also gave her an opportunity to help others. She now had the chance to witness to other widows, other women who had experienced loss. Now she could share her testimony that God is loving and strong, compassionate and merciful.

God gives each of us a second chance for our grief

too. We don't have to wallow in it. We don't have to deny it. When we grieve for our children, when we suffer and struggle, God tells us how to use our grief to help others.

8. Read 2 Corinthians 1:3–4.

How can you comfort someone who is in pain?

I think of Lindy, who learned that Finley's extra chromosome is actually a blessing. Lindy uses the pain she felt in that hospital room to encourage other moms who struggle with this same diagnosis for their own children.

In our grief, we can share in a similar message. Like a widowed woman who lost her son two thousand years ago, we learn that God isn't finished with us. In our pain, He meets us with His grace and helps us through it. He comes to us and offers us life.

Our response as His children? To praise Him.

Our response as women, as His daughters? To share our stories.

This is how God designed us as women. He's given us the ability to comfort one another, to nurture sisters who are in pain, to inspire others through our relationships. God has given women unique abilities to care. Amen? Amen!

Let's celebrate those abilities. Let's share our stories as testimonies to lift up our sisters in Christ, to show them that God is good. He is not finished with any of us.

WIDOW OF NAIN • THE GRIEVING MOM

What is your testimony? God's sovereignty means "for those who love God all things work for good" (Romans 8:28). This means that while you don't want to let your pain define you, it certainly can become your story. As women, our grief becomes our way to relate to others, our way to tell them that God isn't finished with them yet.

God Loves the Grieving Mom

When I told a friend that the widow of Nain was the last mom in this study, she groaned. "Really? Too bad you're ending with such a depressing one. She's the bitter end, huh?"

Fair enough. It is a story about a widow, and that fact doesn't change.

But my friend wasn't thinking about how happily her story ends. Jesus raises this woman's son from the dead! This bereft mom gets what so many of us ask God for. She can hear her son talk again. She can feel his hug and live the rest of her own life in joy. She gets to see the living, breathing God perform the most amazing miracle.

This miracle wasn't just for her and her son. This is a miracle for each of us. The fact that Christ Jesus conquered death is the ultimate hope for us as humans. From our first mom, Eve—whose story ushered sin and death and destruction into the world—to the widow who watched the Messiah, promised to Eve and to every mother, command death to disappear.

As mothers, we're so vulnerable to pain. Our children's choices and circumstances can catapult us into a hurt so deep, we feel we can never escape. At those moments, we can look to Jesus Christ, who is compassionate, who knows the depth of pain we feel.

No matter what struggles we face as mothers, we can always look to God's power of redemption.

9. a. Read Galatians 3:14. What has God given us?

   b. Read Philippians 1:6.

      What promise of hope does God give us?

   c. Read 2 Corinthians 12:9–10.

      What can we do in our struggles?

Pray

Lord, strengthen me to trust Your promises, to live out my faith, to share my story. Help me turn to You in all my struggles. Help me share Your message of hope and eternal life through my testimony. In Your Son's name I pray. Amen.

Leader's Notes

Session 1, Eve: The Forgiven Mom

1. a. Not to eat of it or he would die.

    b. She disobeyed God and ate from the tree of knowledge of good and evil.

    c. She wanted to be like God.

2. She could be like God and know good and evil.

3. They were suddenly aware of their nakedness, of their humanness.

4. Answers will vary, but may include: To be independent of God is to be human, to experience the world separated from God's holiness. To be independent of our perfect God is to know sin.

5. She would experience pain in childbirth. Her husband would rule over her.

6. Jesus, our Redeemer.

7. "I have gotten a man with the help of the LORD."

8. Grace. Because of Jesus Christ, all God's children have righteousness and eternal life.

9. Her son Cain killed his brother Abel.

10. To God.

11. Jesus Christ, the promised Redeemer, would be his descendant. We see here that Jesus would be a descendant of Eve too.

12. Our sins are scarlet.

13. He forgives us so we're white as snow.
    We're completely forgiven.

14. We turn to God. He wipes out our sin.
    Forgiveness refreshes us.

15. Answers will vary.

16. "Be kind to one another, tenderhearted, forgiving one another, as God in Christ forgave you."

17. "Therefore, if anyone is in Christ, he is a new creation. The old has passed away, the new has come."

Session 2, Sarah: The Insecure Mom

1. Sarah was Abraham's wife. God had promised Abraham a great nation, a nation He would bless. Sarah was barren. She had no children.

2. Sarah was well past her childbearing years.

3. Sarah is silent. Through her husband's betrayal and her terrifying days as Pharaoh's wife, she appears graceful under pressure.

4. Answers will vary.

5. Several valuable animals.

6. To command such a large tribe, Sarah must have been very competent.

7. She must have felt so much pressure to do her part in His plan.

8. Marriage meant that one man and one woman should become one flesh.

9. Sarah's sin hurt her relationship with Abraham. It hurt Hagar. It was a sin against God.

10. Sarah would bear a son, Isaac.

11. He reminds believers that it's through Christ we have access to God's promises, and that those promises are for each of us personally.

12. Answers will vary.

Session 3, Hagar: The Picked-On Mom

1. Answers will vary.

2. Abraham and Sarah don't call her by name.

Sarah commands her to have sex with her husband.

3. Answers may vary, but may include: Hagar probably didn't want to have sex with Abraham. Here we see that her desires didn't matter.

4. Marriage and sex should be between one man and one woman.

5. Hagar must have suddenly felt so important.

6. Hagar was prideful. She now hated Sarah.

7. a. No. Sarah complained to Abraham about Hagar's contempt toward her.
   b. He gave her permission to deal harshly with Hagar.
   c. Hagar ran away.

8. The Lord gave Hagar water, direction, a promise, a name for her son, and insight into her son's character.

9. Answers will vary but should include that God was gracious to continue her pregnancy; to listen to her affliction; to give this runaway water, direction, and hope.

10. To Hagar, this was probably encouraging.

11. a. "You are a God of seeing."
    b. God saw her. He saw her for who she was, and He cared for her.

12. As sinners, we're completely hopeless. Jesus is our answer for eternal life.

13. Abraham could teach Ishmael about the Lord.

14. There was surely lots of friction between the women. Hagar had given birth to Abraham's firstborn son, so the women competed against one another.

15. Sarah gave birth to Isaac, and they circumcised him. Even though God told Abraham that Isaac was the promised child, Sarah was insecure and threatened by Ishmael and Hagar.

16. To Sarah, this other child threatened Isaac's inheritance.

17. God would bless him, multiply his descendants, and make him a great nation.
18. Abraham was worried about Ishmael.
19. a. "What troubles you, Hagar?"
    God is compassionate to her.
    b. "Up! Lift up the boy."
    c. God gives her water to ensure her survival.
20. a–d. Answers will vary.

Session 4, Rebekah: The Skeptical Mom

1. a. His beloved wife, Sarah, Isaac's mother, has died.
   b. You will have descendants more numerous than the stars.
   c. Isaac needs a wife, a woman from Paddan-aram, their home country.
   d. A woman from Paddan-aram may not want to come to Canaan, the land that God has promised to His people.
   e. He prays for God to lead him to the right woman by giving him a sign. She'll be the woman who offers to water his camels.
2. She's not only from Paddan-aram, but she's also from Abraham's own family. She's Isaac's relative.
3. He bows his head and gives thanksgiving to God for answering his prayer.
4. Through Christ Jesus, He will provide everything we need. Our real treasure is faith in our Savior.
5. Praise and thanksgiving.
6. She willingly leaves her family to follow God's command.
7. Isaac loved Rebekah.
8. Isaac had heard about and seen the pain that Abraham's polygamy caused. God eventually provided a miracle for his mother and father. This surely led Isaac to pray for a

miracle and to trust God.

9. a. He prays for Rebekah to conceive a child.

    b. He blesses Rebekah and Isaac by allowing Rebekah to conceive twins.

10. She turns to God in prayer.

11. Esau.

12. These parents showed favoritism and disagreement.

13. There was a famine, and Isaac and Rebekah had to move their family to Gerar. Isaac, like his father, did not have faith in God's protection and lied to the king that Rebekah was his sister. Esau married two Hittite women, openly defying the Lord and his family's faith.

14. Answers may vary, but may include: as she watched her husband's lack of faith and her son's lack of faith, she would have wondered if God would provide for her— especially when she and her family were hungry.

15. He sells his birthright for a bowl of stew.

16. She helps Jacob trick her loyal husband into giving the blessing to her favorite son.

17. God would have accomplished His plan with or without Rebekah's help. Regardless of Isaac's actions, her sin is skepticism because she doesn't trust.

18. He wants to kill Jacob in revenge for stealing his blessing.

19. She sends Jacob away to her brother Laban.

20. He's there at least twenty years, much longer than Rebekah could have ever imagined.

21. His divine nature is in His creation, including His creation of humans. God's fingerprints are all over, for anyone to see and believe.

22. Those of us who, deep down, know that God exists, but don't honor Him. We claim to be wise, but we're missing the most important wisdom.

23. God designed us in love. The existence of love in the world is proof that we are intentionally designed by a Creator who loves us.
24. God sent His Son, Jesus, to redeem us. Jesus' ministry was sharing love with others.
25. We need faith like a child to enter the kingdom of heaven.

Session 5, Jochebed: the Faithful Mom

1. a. Her family had passed their faith down from generation to generation.
   b. Her faith was part of who she was. It was natural for her to teach her kids about their Lord.
   c. Moses, Aaron, and Miriam.
2. She must have been an example of steadfast faith in God to raise such faithful kids.
3. The Hebrews were enslaved by the Egyptians.
4. The Egyptians forced them to do difficult manual labor.
5. a. He commanded them to kill all the male newborn babies.
   b. They claimed the Hebrews were too strong to need midwives.
   c. He commanded them to throw all the newborn males into the Nile River.
6. a. She does place Moses in the river, but she puts him in a waterproof basket.
   b. She nursed her own baby. She was paid for it. She cared for Moses the first three years of his life.
   c. She taught him to love and fear the Lord.
   d. The inheritance of faith. She must have prayed with him, praised God with him, and taught him about his faithful ancestors.
7. Despite the horrific oppression, Jochebed trusted God.

8. She watches for Moses, surely praying as she waited. She runs to get her mother so Jochebed can nurse him.

9. Answers will vary.

10. Moses would go on to lead his family's people to escape Pharaoh, the oppressor.

11. Answers will vary.

12. He promises He will never leave us or forsake us.

13. Teach God's commands to your children.

14. Diligently, and by all we say and do.

15. The fruit of the Spirit are love, joy, peace, patience, kindness, goodness, faithfulness, gentleness, and self-control.

16. To "proclaim the excellencies of Him who called you out of darkness into His marvelous light."

Session 6, Ruth: The Blended-Family Mom

1. The Moabites descended from the incestuous relationship between Lot and his oldest daughter.

2. He sacrifices his oldest son as a burnt offering.

3. About ten years.

4. Her sons were married but to Moabite women. Despite a famine in Bethlehem, her family was able to live for another ten years. She had two daughters-in-law that she loved. Her sons and husband died. She had to move back to Bethlehem, where she had no money and no land. She had to send Orpah back to her pagan family and gods, but Ruth chose to stay with her.

5. Follow Naomi. Follow God. Stay committed to Naomi and God until death.

6. Orpah chooses to go back to her people. Ruth promises to leave Moab and move to Bethlehem, God's country.

7. a. She's made a personal confirmation of God, not as her family's God, but as her own.

215

b. Like Ruth, today's confirmand publicly confesses faith in the Lord God and agreement with His Word.

8. Her loyal daughter-in-law, Ruth, was with her. It was the beggining of the barley harvest, which meant the famine was over.

9. a. He was a respected landowner who treated Ruth well.

b. "The LORD repay you for what you have done, and a full reward be given you by the LORD, the God of Israel, under whose wings you have come to take refuge!"

c. By showing God's love to Ruth, they are showing her that the Lord is the God of love.

10. a. She went to the barley fields and gathered the left-overs that the harvesters didn't pick up.

b. She worked from early in the morning until late in the evening with only a short rest.

c. Boaz offers her protection from the other workers. He asks her to stay in his field. He invites Ruth to eat with him. She takes home a significant amount of barley to Naomi.

11. To be great, you must be a servant. Even Jesus, the Son of Man, did not come to be served but to serve.

12. She is trustworthy. She brings good, not harm. Her character is steady. She is reliable and dependable. She doesn't settle for mediocre. She works hard. She is practical. People can depend on her. She is responsible. She is a generous servant. She is wise and trusts God.

13. Because Ruth's husband, Mahlon, had died, she could marry a kinsman-redeemer to buy back the land of Naomi's family.

14. a. Naomi tells Ruth to prepare herself like a bride and then go to the threshing floor. There, she should lie at Boaz's feet and ask him to cover her. This would be like a modern-day proposal.

    b. When Ruth chooses to marry Boaz, she chooses family. He is Naomi's relative, so this marriage will buy Naomi's land back for her and keep it in the family. Boaz is also a believer in Yahweh and has shared his faith with Ruth.

15. Peace that surpasses human understanding.

16. Ruth is married to Boaz, an honorable man of God. Naomi is cared for, and she has a grandson to care for. Ruth, a convert from a pagan lifestyle, is now a believer in the one true God. God blesses Ruth and Boaz with a child, Obed, who will be the grandfather to King David, Israel's powerful and godly king.

17. Like clay jars, we're easily broken. We carry the life and death of Jesus Christ in us.

18. We are all His brothers and sisters in heaven.

Session 7, Hannah: The Single-Minded Mom

1. a. She demanded her servant, Hagar, sleep with her husband.
   b. She claimed she would die, and she also gave her servant to her husband.

2. She couldn't eat. Her face was downcast. Her husband worried about her.

3. They took the best meats from sacrifices for themselves. They committed fornication with women at the tabernacle.

4. The tabernacle was where she went to be with her Lord.

5. Hannah tells him that she is not drunk; she is pouring her soul out to the Lord.

6. Eli gives Hannah the blessing that God will grant her request for a baby.

7. She believed it so strongly that she was no longer depressed. She was able to eat again. Her anguish was

over. She fully trusted God.

8. Hannah vowed that she would give her son to the Lord and that she would not cut his hair.

9. He loved and supported Hannah, even though it would mean giving up his son.

10. Even though she would give her son to God, she also cared deeply for him. She was a responsible mother.

11. God loves a cheerful giver. He loves when we give first to Him. He delights in our praise and in our gifts.

12. She prays a remarkable worship song to God.

13. Hannah describes her God as her strength, holiness, a rock, the God of knowledge.

14. Answers may vary, but should include: Our sinful nature always disappoints us. The Lord raises us up.

15. He will guard the feet of the faithful.

16. God also blessed Hannah with more children.

17. Both women are amazed God chose humble, ordinary women like them. Both women rejoice. Hannah proclaims, "My heart exalts in the LORD" (1 Samuel 2:1). In Luke 1:47, Mary praises, "My spirit rejoices in God my Savior." Both women sing praises of who God is.

18. "The fruit of the Spirit is love, joy, peace, patience, kindness, goodness, faithfulness, gentleness, self-control."

19. Sacrifice your self for Christ. If you save your "self," you lose Jesus.

20. Through Christ, we can keep our eyes focused on the examples we have. We view our lives through the lens of faith.

21. We have life and peace through Christ.

Session 8, Bathsheba: The Flexible Mom

1. Bathsheba was very beautiful; she was bathing (purifying

herself after menstruation); her house was close to the palace, so she had probably met David before; she had sex with the king even though she was married; she was pregnant with his child.

2. Her husband was a faithful soldier, away at war. David brought this noble man back and tried to trick him into sleeping with his wife to pass the pregnancy off as his. When Uriah wouldn't comply, David made sure he was killed in battle. Bathsheba mourned.

3. When David sends a messenger for Bathsheba, she goes to him and has sex.

4. David demands the rich man should die and restore the lamb fourfold—be punished four times over.

5. She must have rejoiced in this new baby, who was beloved of the Lord.

6. You shall not murder. You shall not commit adultery. You shall not steal. You shall not bear false witness against your neighbor. You shall not covet your neighbor's wife. Essentially, they have broken all of them.

7. Answers will vary, but may include: Adultery breaks up marriages; when you lie, you lose someone's trust; making other things more important than God always disappoints us; coveting other peoples' lives will only leave us unfulfilled.

8. When confronted by Nathan.

9. Forgiveness of our sins and real peace.

10. A relationship with God through Christ.

11. Through God's Word, Sacrament, prayer, and His forgiveness.

12. She reminded David of his promise that Solomon would be king. David clearly respected her opinion.

13. Through Christ, we have a clean heart; a renewed, right spirit; the Holy Spirit; joy in salvation; and a willing spirit.

LEADER'S NOTES

Session 9, Elizabeth: The Mentoring Mom

1. She was from the daughters of Aaron. Both she and her husband, Zechariah, were old. They were also "righteous before God, walking blamelessly in all the commandments and statues of the Lord."

2. She was barren. Both she and her husband were advanced in years.

3. a. A baby.

    b. How could God give them a baby since both he and Elizabeth were old?

    c. Because of Zechariah's skeptical question, he wouldn't be able to speak until the promised baby was born.

4. a. God would perform a miracle through Mary's fertility also. She would be pregnant, even though she was a virgin.

    b. By Elizabeth's pregnancy. It was her sixth month.

    c. Even her old relative, Elizabeth, is pregnant.

5. Even though it was a long trip from Nazareth to Jerusalem, Mary hurried to Elizabeth's house in the hill country to visit her cousin. They were both friends and relatives.

6. When John hears Mary's greeting, he leaps in Elizabeth's womb. Through the Holy Spirit, Elizabeth realizes that Mary is carrying the Christ Child.

7. She burst into her praise song, the Magnificat.

8. John would be great before the Lord, he would not drink strong drink, he would be filled with the Holy Spirit, he would prepare the world for a Savior.

9. They rejoiced with her at the miracle of her son, born to her in old age.

10. According to the covenant of circumcision, they brought him to be dedicated to God through circumcision. They were devout believers.

11. Zechariah and Elizabeth followed Gabriel's instructions in verse 13. Because they were old, God showed His favor by having Elizabeth conceive.

12. God is giving them salvation through His promised Redeemer. John is the prophet who will teach about the Redeemer.

13. To prepare the world for the Messiah.

14. He told the people to repent. He reprimanded the Pharisees and Sadducees. He baptized crowds and even baptized Jesus.

15. They should be reverent in behavior. They should teach what is good and train the young women to love their husbands and children; to be self-controlled; to be pure, hard workers; to be kind; and to be submissive to their husbands.

16. "Be imitators of me, as I am of Christ."

17. Answers will vary.

18. By "speaking the truth in love," and by continually studying Scripture for better understanding.

Session 10, Mary: The Accepting Mom

1. A virgin, in the city of David (Bethlehem).

2. She didn't understand. She was a humble woman, so she didn't think she deserved God's special favor.

3. "Behold, I am a servant of the Lord; let it be to me according your word."

4. We will be humbled. But if we humble ourselves, God will exalt us.

5. He chose you. You are His.

6. a. Zechariah asks, "How shall I know this? For I am an old man, and my wife is advanced in years." He demands proof that God can do what He says He'll do.

   b. Mary asks, "How will this be since I am a virgin?"

   c. Mary's asking how this will work logistically, or what her part in God's work will be.

7. a. Answers may vary, but should include: God would protect her throughout the trials she would have as Jesus' mother.

   b. God protects us. We can trust Him. He has promised to shield us.

8. a. His mightiness and His holiness.

   b. God's mercy.

   c. God's power.

   d. God's goodness.

   e. God's faithfulness.

9. a. Jesus was the world's salvation. He was a light for the Gentiles and would mean glory for Israel.

   b. A sword will pierce your own soul also.

10. Hurt, confusion, sadness. Perhaps she expected this and understood, but she still would have missed her Son.

11. a. Perhaps she felt pain to see her innocent, perfect Son die a tortured death.

   b. Joy to know He had completed His promises. She must have felt so loved that He was deeply concerned about her care.

12. After His ascension, she is praying with the other disciples.

13. For good works, which God prepared beforehand.

14. He works in the lives of believers to further His kingdom.

Session 11, Eunice and Lois: The Nurturing Moms

1. a. They believed Paul and Barnabas were Greek gods. They tried to worship them.

   b. They tore their clothing to show they were horrified.

   c. The Jews from the surrounding areas stoned Paul.

2. Timothy, his son, was not circumcised.

3. God is clear: any male believer had to be circumcised when he was eight days old.

4. Paul circumcises Timothy. The Jewish people may not have accepted God's Word from someone different from them.

5. When believers attach themselves to unbelievers, they're unequal. They don't see life with the same hope.

6. a. God's Word.

    b. When Satan intercepts God's Word.

    c. The hearts of those who shallowly accept God's Word.

    d. The hearts of those who accept God's Word but allow worldly concerns, like money, to choke it.

    e. Those who hear the word and truly understand it, causing it to bear fruit.

7. Timothy's father, Eunice's husband, wasn't a believer. The family lived in a pagan community.

8. "My beloved child."

9. a. "I have fought the good fight, I have finished the race, I have kept the faith. Henceforth there is laid up for me the crown of righteousness, which the Lord, the righteous judge, will award to me on that Day, and not only to me but also to all who have loved His appearing."

    b. Ministry is filled with hard times. But in the end, we know that God's crown of righteousness is the best reward.

10. We have God's words in our hearts and our souls. We should teach them to our children all the time.

11. If we train them in the kingdom of God when they're young, they'll remember it when they're older.

12. When kids are young, they are less cynical and more open to believe they were created by a loving God. Children understand better that God's grace is a free gift for us.

13. a. By taking them to church, reading the Bible to them,

and encouraging them to be part of a community that models faith.

b. A peaceful and righteous heart.

14. You can tell someone's heart by what he or she invests in.

Session 12, The Widow of Nain: The Grieving Mom

1. To visit widows and orphans and help them.
2. a. Her only son had died.

   b. She was left completely alone. On her way to bury her son, a large crowd was with her. This was a community tragedy.
3. He healed those who were sick, lame, and demon-possessed.
4. He feels compassion. He tells the widow not to cry.
5. a. "The harvest is plentiful, but the laborers are few."

   b. Answers will vary, but should include: The world we live in—full of hurting souls—is the harvest. Christians are the laborers.
6. He has called us according to His purpose. Even in our struggles, we can trust that all things work for the good of those who love God.
7. a. Our world is full of sin, so we'll have difficulties. But He has already conquered this world.

   b. Through our hard times, we develop our Christian character. We learn to rely on God.

   c. Christ's strength.
8. God comforts us, so we can show that same comfort to others.
9. a. The Holy Spirit, through our redemption through Jesus Christ.

   b. God will complete His work when all believers are with Him in heaven.

   c. Rely on God, who has delivered us.